2022 M2 Chip Powered

MacBook Air

User Guide

A Comprehensive 2022 M2 Chip MacBook Air User
Manual with Tips and Tricks

Stanley Lindberg

Copyright

Table of Contents

v

Introduction

The 2022 MacBook Air has a whole new look, an upgraded M2 CPU, and a notched display. While it more closely resembles the design of the MacBook Pro, it is still the same ultra-thin and light laptop we have come to adore, but with a steep price.

The new, very thin MacBook Air comes in four gorgeous finishes and has a more prominent 13.6-inch Liquid Retina display, a 1080p HD camera, MagSafe charging, and other features.

Additionally, M2 adds 24GB of quick unified memory, ProRes acceleration, and up to 20 hours of battery life. The general aesthetic is quite similar to the current MacBook Pro models. Although the corners of the device have a somewhat flat appearance, they are not as thick as those of the MacBook Pro. When you take up the MacBook Air, you'll instantly note how small it is—it measures only a hair over 11 millimeters.

Two Thunderbolt ports and a MagSafe power input are located on the left side, whereas the only connector on the right is a headphone jack. Even while there aren't many connectors, you do get an additional Thunderbolt port to use while the tablet is charging thanks to the inclusion of MagSafe.

The MacBook Air 2022 model does away with the speaker grille on the laptop's lid, choosing instead tiny speaker grilles in the hinge and beneath the keyboard, in contrast to the MacBook Pro and previous-generation MacBook Air.

Features of the MacBook Air 2022

Released earlier this year, the MacBook Air 2022 comes with a whole lot of new features that benefit users all around. The features include the following:

Liquid Retina Display

Apple upgraded the MacBook Air's display with a bigger Liquid Retina screen. Instead of using a single big backlight panel, the screen employs numerous LEDs, which results in a brighter display with deeper blacks and more vivid colors. Due to lower bezels, the screen size was also increased from 13.3 to 13.6 inches, eliminating space for the conventional FaceTime camera.

M2 Processor

The 2022 MacBook Air is equipped with the M2 chip, the most recent Apple CPU. The M2 is a System on a Chip (SoC) kind of processor, meaning that it combines the CPU, GPU, RAM, and other components onto one single chip.

Since the M2 has 25% more transistors than the M1, its upgraded CPU operates at a rate about 1.4 times quicker than the M1. (A CPU can manage more simultaneous operations with more transistors.) Although 2022 MacBook Airs still start at 8GB, it is designed to run more programs concurrently with 50% greater maximum RAM capacity — from 16GB to 24GB.

The GPU now renders graphics at speeds of up to 35% quicker. The cost of a 10-core GPU, which replaces the eight cores in the standard M2 model, is $300. With three times quicker video transcoding, Apple's new media engine is also optimized for ProRes and ProRes RAW, two well-known high-end video codecs.

The M2 is up to 15 times quicker than computers with Intel Core i5 processors for anybody having a MacBook Air, even from a year earlier than 2020.

Substantial redesign

Like the M1, the M2 takes up less room since it doesn't need a fan to stay cool. To accommodate the fanless CPU, Apple redesigned the 2022 MacBook Air, giving it the appearance of a smaller MacBook Pro without a wedge up front. Compared to the previous generation, it is both lighter and slimmer.

Instead of the shorter **function keys** on the previous version, the top row of keys on the keyboard is now the same height as the rest. The Touch ID module's size is also increased as a result.

Since 2022 will see the return of MagSafe charging, charging will no longer occupy one of the two

Thunderbolt (USB 4) ports. You can connect to your iPhone without using a second wall adapter with the $1,499 Air with the 10-core GPU since it has a plug featuring an additional USB-C port. The 2022 MacBook Air comes in four colors, including the traditional silver and Space Gray, as well as Starlight (a pure gold) and Midnight (black).

Improved audio

With four spatial speakers—two more than the previous generation, FaceTime conversations now sound better on the MacBook Air. High-impedance headphones are now also supported through the headphone jack. That indicates that the port has sufficient power to support studio-quality, wired headphones.

1080p FaceTime camera

The FaceTime camera on the device has been upgraded to full HD, or 1080p (1,920 x 1,080 pixels) quality. This is a significant improvement over 720p and offers more detailed visuals during video chats.

Display

The 2022 MacBook Air has a bigger 13.6-inch display than the 2020 model, which has a 13.3-inch display. As opposed to the Retina display from the previous generation, the new display uses Apple's most recent Liquid Retina technology. The corners are rounded rather than square, which is the most obvious change on the 2022 MacBook Air. The more expensive Liquid Retina XDR screens are seen in the 14-inch and 16-inch MacBook Pro models.

The M2 MacBook Air is 25% brighter than the M1 MacBook Air, which has a maximum brightness of 400 nits. This puts the Air on par with the 13-inch MacBook Pro but much behind the 1,000 nits of the XDR display. The ProMotion technology of previous versions is absent from the MacBook Air.

The M2 MacBook Air continues the pattern started by Apple with the MacBook Pro, which had a screen notch for the camera. The camera notch goes all the way to the menu bar, and the bezels surrounding the screen are very tiny compared to the earlier model (but still not as thin as the 14-inch and 16-

inch MacBook Pro). Since the screen size is larger, thanks to the notch, you have an extra usable area. The menu bar's bottom portion maintains its previous 16:10 aspect ratio.

Charging

The M2 MacBook Air's battery life is identical to that of the M1 model, but you can charge it more quickly. The $1,499 variant adds a new 35W Dual USB-C Port Compact Power Adapter for charging two devices simultaneously, in contrast to the basic model's conventional 30W USB-C Power Adapter.

Chapter 1

When you power up the new MacBook Air 2022 for the first time, Setup Assistant guides you through the straightforward procedures required to begin using your device. You can opt to follow all the instructions or skip some and come back to them later. After initial setup, it could make sense, for instance, to set up Screen Time, which you can establish for various users.

How to set up the MacBook Air (2022)

The steps include:

1. Take the device out of the box and proceed to unpack the other accessories.

2. Double-check that you have a laptop, charging cord, and power supply readily available.

3. Disconnect the computer from the power adapter, insert the USB-C port into the adapter, and then plug in the MagSafe adaptor. The power button can be found on the MacBook Air (2022)'s top right corner when the lid is opened. It also serves as your Touch ID button.

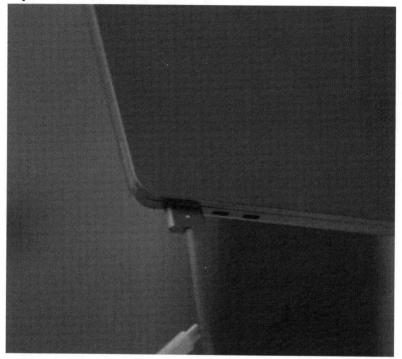

Setting up the macOS Monterey on MacBook Air 2022

1. After a little delay, macOS Monterey 12.5 should start up and say **"Hello"** to you in various languages on the screen.

2. The Setup Assistant will welcome and guide you through each step.
3. Select your preferred language, geographic location, time zone, and any accessibility features you want to activate.

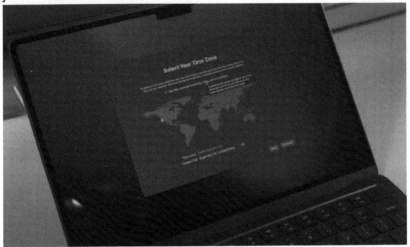

4. Proceed to create a Wi-Fi connection or choose a different option, like your cellular network.
5. The Migration Assistant will make it easier to move data from older Macs or Windows PCs.
6. If you don't already have an Apple ID, you can create one after this and select to **sign in**.
7. You have to accept the T&C. Your name, account name, and password will then be set up.
8. After following the instructions, you'll be prompted to set up **Touch ID**.

9. To accomplish this, press the **power button** in the top right corner with your finger (this is optional, you can skip it, but it is recommended.)

Create an Apple ID

With an Apple ID, you can access the iTunes Store, App Store, Apple Books, iCloud, FaceTime, and other Apple services. It consists of a password and an email address, such as David cavanna@icloud.com. Either your existing email address or a randomly created @icloud email address can be used to establish an Apple ID.

Create an Apple ID using either your existing email address or the one obtained by iCloud:

1. Open the Apple menu on your MacBook Air 2022, choose **System Preferences**, and then click **Sign In**.

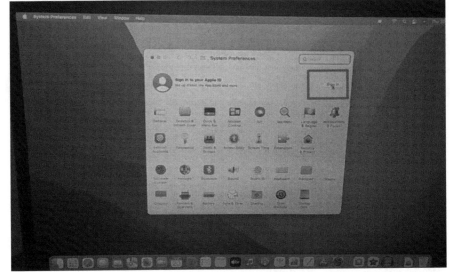

2. Select **Create Apple ID**, then adhere to the prompts on the screen.

3. Type in your billing and payment card details, then click **Continue**.

4. Verify your email address by checking your inbox for a verification email from Apple.

Using your new Apple ID to login into the App Store and other Apple services like iCloud is possible when you confirm your email address. **Note**: You can create an Apple ID without an email address in a variety of nations and locations.

Change Apple ID Password on MacBook Air 2022

It is advised to use a strong password with the Apple ID. Whether it's Apple Music, iCloud, the App Store, or iMessage, you can access the vast array of applications and services in the Apple ecosystem with your Apple ID. However, it is simple for anybody to have their Apple ID password compromised due to the always-developing cyber threats.

Since this is the case, you should learn how to change your Apple ID password by following the steps below.

The steps:

1. Go to "**System Preferences**" on your MacBook Air 2022 and choose the "**Apple ID**" tile.

2. After that, choose **"Password & Security"** and then **"Change Password."**

3. This is where you must input the passcode for your MacBook Air 2022.

4. Next, input the new password in case the previous one was compromised or you forgot it. To confirm and verify the new secure Apple ID password, enter it again.

5. The new password should be available when you click the **"Change"** button.

Choose your Apple ID Image

You can choose from a picture, Memoji, emoji, or other images to set your Apple ID. Your user login image and **My Card** in Contacts both use your Apple ID photo.

The steps:

1. Click **Apple ID** 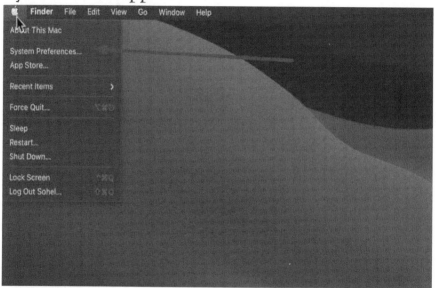 under **System Preferences** on your Mac's Apple menu.

2. Click **Sign In** and provide your Apple ID credentials. Then follow the directions shown on the screen.
3. In the sidebar, click the image that appears close to your name.

4. From there, carry out any of the below options:

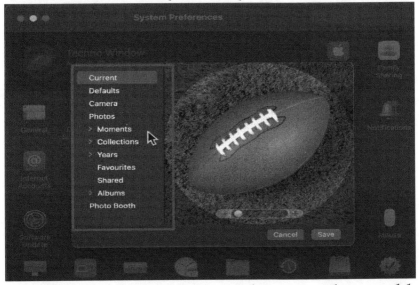

- **Choosing a Memoji:** To choose and assemble a face picture, click Memoji and then the **Add button** ⊕. Alternatively, select an Memoji on the list and then pick a position and style you prefer.

- **Choosing an emoji**: Click **Emoji**, then choose an image from the emoji library by clicking the **Add button** ⊕. Alternatively, choose an emoji from the list and a style.

- **Decide on a monogram**: Choose a background color, click **Monogram**, and then type initials.

- **Capture a photo using your Mac's camera**: Press **Camera**. After you've set up your shot, press the **Camera button**.

- **Pick a picture from your Photos gallery**: Choose **Photos**. Click the arrow ❯ next to Photos in the sidebar, choose the desired album, and then click a picture to see images from that album.

- **Decide on a recommended picture**: After clicking Suggestions, choose a photo.

5. You can change an image's appearance after choosing it. Attempt one of the following:
   - **Modify the image's position**: Move the image around the circle.
   - Drag the slider left or right to zoom in or out.

6. Hit **Save**.

Chapter 2

Set Up and Use Time Machine

Apple offers a backup solution for Macs called Time Machine. It produces a straightforward **"image" or "snapshot"** of your MacBook Air 2022, which is just a compressed file with everything on your Mac at the time of the backup that you can restore when necessary. You can refresh your Mac after restoring it to factory settings or use Time Machine backups to boot a new device.

It's quite easy to set up Time Machine. This is how:

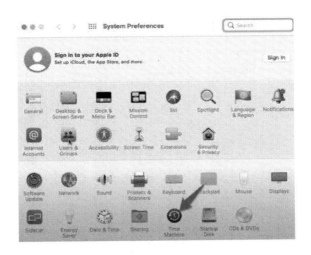

1. Click .

2. From the drop-down menu, choose "**System Preferences.**"
3. Select "**Time Machine.**"

Note: Following these instructions will teach you how to configure automatic backups in Time Machine.

1. On the **Time Machine's** window left side, click "**Automatic Backups.**"
2. Pick the disk that will house your backups.

On a predetermined schedule, Time Machine will start producing a backup to the disk you've chosen.

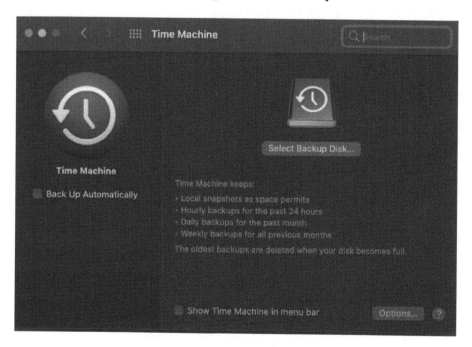

How to repair MacBook Air 2022 with Time Machine

It's simple to restore a Mac from a Time Machine backup, but it's not always the best choice. Restoring from a backup may cause your Mac to take days to restart. Think about how much time you have to dedicate to that procedure. There is also little likelihood that **Time Machine** will improve in this area since Apple no longer manufactures the AirPort Time Capsule.

Disk Drill is a good option because it effortlessly retrieves lost files—or at least files you thought you'd lost. You may be able to locate those missing files with **Disk Drill** rather than having to spend hours recovering your Mac only to retrieve one file by digging through Time Machine backups:

1. In Disk Drill, choose the disk that contains the data you lost.
2. Select "**Find lost data.**"
3. Examine the results when the scan is finished and choose the files you wish to restore.

4. Select "**Recover.**"

The following instructions will show you how to restore all the files and app data from your previous backup if you do need to go back there:

1. Restart your computer while it is linked to your backup drive.
2. As the Mac starts up, hold down **Command + R** to enter Recovery Mode.
3. After you see the Apple logo, let go of the keys.
4. Select "**Restore from Time Machine backup**" in the Disk Utility menu and **Continue**.
5. Select the restore source you want, then click **Continue**.
6. If asked, enter the admin password and click **Continue** again.
7. Choose the backup you wish to restore (by date), and then choose the backup's destination.
8. Select "**Restore.**"

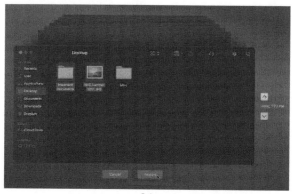

9. Then restart your MacBook Air.

Alternatively, you can transfer data from your Time Machine backup to Mac using Migration Assistant (included in **Applications > Utilities**).

How to recover data from a Mac using Time Machine

Here is how to accomplish it:

1. Check that your MacBook Air 2022 is linked to your backup drive. Make sure your router is configured and your computer is connected to the same network if you're using a **Time Capsule**. Your backup drive will immediately "**connect**" to your Mac via this option.
2. When asked how you'd want to transfer your data, choose "**From a Mac, Time Machine backup, or startup disk**" when logging into your MacBook Air 2022.
3. Choose your backup disk from the available options on the next screen.
4. Select "**Continue.**"
5. After selecting the data you want to transmit, click **Continue**.

Create and Remove Partitions

You could consider partitioning your Mac's hard disk to create distinct containers for various data since newer Mac models provide more capacity. Using this, you might run an entirely new operating system on one Mac disk or keep your personal and professional data separate.

How Do Partitions Work?

It's critical to understand what a partition is before learning how to partition an HDD or SSD. To put it simple, a partition is a designated area on a hard disk that is set apart from the others. Even though it's still the same physical disk, this keeps the whole partition isolated from other partitions on your hard drive or solid-state drive.

How to Create a New Partition on a Mac's Disk

In macOS Monterey, creating a new partition is simple. The internal storage system and any external storage devices attached to your Mac must follow these instructions.

To ensure that you are safeguarded against any unintended data loss, it is a good practice to back up your data before making any changes to disk partitions.

How to partition a hard drive in macOS Monterey:

1. Launch **Mac's Disk Utility**. This can be done by using Spotlight to look for it or by going to **Finder > Applications > Utilities**.

2. In the left-hand sidebar, you can view all of your accessible storage volumes. These are mentioned under their respective topics and include both internal and external volumes.

3. After choosing which disk to partition, choose **Partition**.

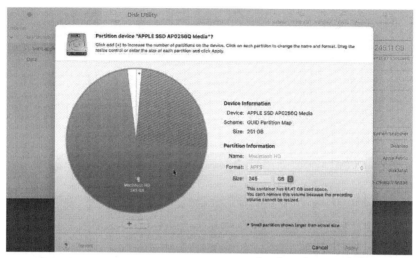

4. To create a new partition, click the **addition (+) symbol** on the storage allocation screen. The volume you choose cannot be partitioned if it is inaccessible, which most likely means that it is full or that the drive is protected.

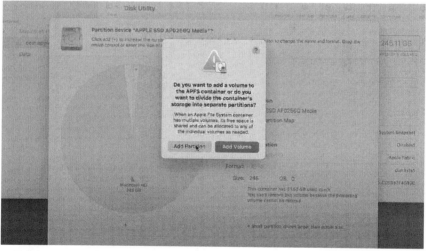

5. Give your new partition a name and decide on a format for it. Select **APFS** if you're not sure which to go with.

6. Decide on the new partition's size. The entire space will then be divided between the existing partition(s) and the new one you are establishing. The divide can also be expanded or contracted by moving the picture to the left.
7. After you are satisfied with all the information, click **Apply**.

How to Remove a Partition

Disk Utility can be used to remove partitions from your Mac's storage device if it contains several partitions. You can use the extra storage space created by deleting a partition to expand an existing partition.

It's crucial to understand that deleting a partition will first remove all of its stored data before permanently destroying the partition. Make a backup of everything on the partition before deleting it if you want to save all of the data.

Remove a partition:

1. Launch **Mac's Disk Utility**. From the left sidebar, choose the partition you wish to remove.

2. Select the partition you want to remove from the pie chart by clicking the **Partition option** in the top menu.

3. Check that the correct partition is chosen before using the minus (-) button. The pie chart will change to reflect your decision to delete the chosen segment.

4. Select "**Apply.**"

5. A pop-up window will ask for your approval to remove the divider. The partition will be destroyed when you click **Partition** to confirm.

The partition should be successfully erased, freeing up more storage that may be used for other things.

How to Use a Terminal to Erase a Partition

In the majority of cases, managing partitions using Disk Utility should be adequate. However, sometimes Disk Utility won't successfully wipe your partition. You can run into trouble since the partition has to be wiped before it can be deleted from the disk.

Fortunately, you can also totally delete a single partition using Disk Utility after erasing it from the command line via Terminal. Before wiping the partition, make sure you have a backup of any vital data you may have on it, since doing so will wipe everything there.

The steps:

1. Firstly, launch **Terminal** on your Mac.
2. Type **diskutil list** into the command line to see your HDD or SSD partitions.
3. Locate the partition that must be deleted, and note its disk identification,
4. To wipe the partition, use the following command. Substitute or change the identifier at the end with your unique disk identifier.
5. A progress bar will appear in Terminal, which you can use to check on the progress of your partition. The partition has been deleted once you get a success message such as **"Finished erase on disk 3s6."**
6. Use Disk Utility to remove the partition using the methods outlined above to entirely erase it.

How to Update macOS Monetary

To install updates and improvements for Safari and other built-in programs on macOS, use **Software Update**.

The steps:

1. Ensure you back up your MacBook Air 2022 before moving on to the next step.
2. Select **System Preferences** from the Apple menu in the bottom-right corner of your screen.
3. From the **System Preferences** pane, choose **Software Update**.

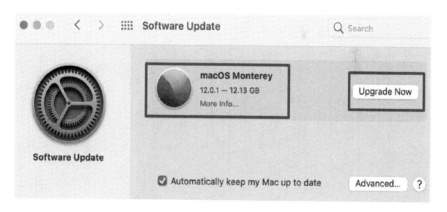

4. Software Update will now look for new software. Check for the following:
   - Click **Update Now or Upgrade Now** to install any new software that Software Update disco-

vers. Restarting or entering an administrator password may be required.

- No new software is presently accessible for your Mac model if Software Update reports that your computer is up-to-date.

If the software update is absent:

- Use Search in the window's corner to look for **"Software Update"** if you don't see a Software Update option in System Preferences.
- If the Software Update feature isn't available for your version of macOS, launch the App Store application, which you can locate in the Dock or your Applications folder. To check for updates, open the **App Store** and click the **Updates tab**.

Chapter 3

How to Sync your iPhone & iPad with Your MacBook Air

You can choose which data to sync between your Mac and the device. You can sync every item of a certain kind (for example, all your movies or photos). Alternatively, you can choose certain things, that give you greater control (for instance, some of your movies and books).

- When you sync your device and Mac, the items are updated once you choose the material you wish to sync.
- You must use a USB or USB-C connection to connect your device to your Mac to set up syncing for the first time. The device symbol appears in the Finder sidebar once you connect it, and choosing the icon shows synchronization choices. Next, you decide what items to sync.

Sync music to your device

1. Connect your device to your MacBook Air 2022. Your device can be connected through Wi-Fi, a USB or USB-C cable, or both.
2. Choose the device from the Finder sidebar in your Mac's Finder.
3. In the button bar, choose **Music**.
4. To enable music synchronization, check the "**Sync music onto [device name]**" box.
5. By checking the option, synchronization is configured to download all of your music to your device.
6. Select "**Selected playlist, artists, albums and genres**" to sync a certain group of songs.
7. Check the box next to each song in the music list that you wish to sync. For each item you don't want to sync, deselect the checkbox. For a list of your material categorized by artists, albums, genres, or playlists, choose the appropriate link.
8. Pick synchronization options:
   - To add videos during synchronizing, check the "**Include videos**" box.
   - To include voice memos while synchronizing, check the "**Include voice memos**" box.

- To have your Mac automatically fill the space on your device with music while synchronizing, check the "**Automatically fill free space with songs**" checkbox. If you don't have enough space to sync your whole music collection to your device but have a large music library on your MacBook Air 2022, choose this option.

9. Click **Apply** when you're ready to sync.

You can decide to automatically sync your Mac and your device every time you connect them. Click the **Eject button** ⏏ in the Finder sidebar before removing your device from your Mac.

Sync Movies to your Device

The steps:

1. Connect your iPhone/iPad to your MacBook Air 2022. Your device can be connected through Wi-Fi, a USB or USB-C cable, or both.
2. Choose the device from the **Finder sidebar** in your Mac's **Finder**. Check if your device doesn't display in the sidebar if you connect your device to your Mac using a USB connection.

3. Select **Movies** from the menu bar.
4. To enable film synchronization, choose the "**Sync films onto [device name]**" checkbox. By checking the option, synchronization is configured to download all your movies to your device.
5. Pick the "**Automatically include**" checkbox, then select the number of recently viewed or unwatched movies from the menu to sync a selection of movies.
6. Tick the boxes next to each movie in the film list that you wish to sync. Uncheck the box next to any movie you don't wish to sync.
7. Click **Apply** when you're ready to sync.

You can decide to automatically sync your MacBook Air and your device every time you connect them. Click the **Eject button** ⏏ in the Finder sidebar before removing your device from your Mac.

Remove Automatically Synced Movies from your Device

Delete the undesired movie from your Mac, and then sync your device to remove it from both your Mac and device. These procedures should be followed if you want to save the movie on your MacBook Air 2022 and get it deleted from your device (iphone/ipad):

1. Connect your device to your MacBook Air 2022. Your device can be connected through Wi-Fi, a USB or USB-C cable, or both.
2. In the Finder on your Mac, click **Movies** in the button bar after choosing your device from the sidebar.
3. Deselect the checkbox next to the movie you want to delete from the list of movies.
4. Then sync your MacBook Air 2022 with the device.

Sync TV Shows between your MacBook Air 2022 and iPhone or iPad

Your Mac's TV programs can be synced to your devices:

The steps:

1. Connect your device to your TV programs. Your device can also be connected through Wi-Fi, a USB or USB-C cable, or both.

2. Choose the device from the Finder sidebar in your Mac's Finder.

3. Select **TV Shows** from the menu bar.

4. To enable TV program synchronization, choose the "**Sync TV programs onto [device name]**" checkbox. By checking the option, synchronization is configured to download all of your TV shows to your device.

5. To sync a selection of TV shows, click the "**Automatically include**" checkbox, then choose the number of the newest, most recent, or oldest unwatched TV shows from the menu. Finally, decide whether to include all or just a few shows from the episode menu.

6. In the TV Programmes list, check the boxes next to each TV show you wish to sync. Uncheck the box next to any TV show you don't want to sync. To see your content arranged by genre, choose Playlists or TV Programs.

7. Click **Apply** when you're ready to sync.

You can decide to automatically sync your Mac and your device every time you connect them. Click the **Eject button** ⏏ in the Finder sidebar before removing your device from your Mac.

Remove TV shows that were automatically synchronized from your device

You can delete the TV show from your Mac and sync your device to erase it from both your Mac and your device.

The procedures below can be used to delete a TV show from only your device while keeping it on your Mac:

1. Connect your device to your MacBook Air 2022.
2. In the Finder 🔍 on your MacBook Air, click **TV Shows** in the button bar after choosing your device from the sidebar.
3. Deselect the checkboxes next to the TV programs you want to remove from the TV Program list.
4. Connect your Mac to your iPad/iPhone.

If you remove an item that syncs automatically from your Mac, it will no longer be available on your device when you next sync. Also, click the **Eject button** ⏏ in the Finder sidebar before removing your device from your Mac.

Synchronize podcasts on your Mac, iPhone, and iPad

You can choose to sync all or any of the podcasts you have downloaded on your Mac to your device. You must sync your iPod with your Mac to add podcasts and other content if you have an iPod classic, iPod nano, or iPod shuffle.

Sync podcasts to your device:

1. First, connect your device to your MacBook Air 2022.
2. Choose the device from the Finder sidebar in your Mac's Finder.
3. Select **Podcasts** from the menu bar.
4. To enable podcast synchronization, check the "**Sync podcasts onto [device name]**" option. When the checkbox is checked, all of your podcasts will be synced to your device.
5. To sync a selection of podcasts, check the "**Automatically copy**" box, then pick the number of most recent, most recent unplayed, or most recent new podcasts from the menu.

6. In the podcasts list, check the boxes next to each podcast you want to synchronize. For any podcast, you don't want to sync, deselect the checkbox.
7. Click **Apply** when you're ready to sync.

Click the **Eject button** ⏏ in the Finder sidebar before removing your device from your Mac.

Remove auto-synced podcasts from your device

Delete the podcast from your Mac, then sync your device to get rid of an undesirable podcast.

Observe these procedures to delete a podcast from only your device while retaining it on your Mac:

1. Connect your device to your MacBook Air 2022. Your device can be connected through Wi-Fi, a USB, or a USB-C cable.
2. In the Finder on your Mac, click on **Podcasts** in the button bar after choosing your device from the sidebar.
3. Uncheck the box next to the podcast you want to delete from the podcast list.

4. Connect your Mac to your device.

If you remove an item that syncs automatically from your Mac, it will no longer be available on your device when you next sync. Also, click the **Eject button** ⏏ in the Finder sidebar before removing your device from your Mac.

Synchronize audiobooks on your Mac, iPhone, and iPad

Your Mac's audiobooks may be synced to your smartphone in whole or in part.

Sync your device with audiobooks:

1. Connect your device to your MacBook Air 2022.
2. Choose the device name from the Finder sidebar in your Mac's Finder.
3. Select **Audiobooks** from the menu bar.
4. To enable audiobook synchronization, check the "**Sync audiobooks onto [device name]**" box. By checking the option, synchronization is configured to download all audiobooks to your device.
5. Select "**Selected audiobooks**" to sync several audiobooks.

6. In the Audiobooks list, check the boxes next to each audiobook you wish to sync. For any audiobooks you don't want to sync, deselect the checkbox.
7. Click Apply when you're ready to sync.

You can decide to automatically sync your Mac and your device every time you connect them. Click the **Eject button** ⏏ in the Finder sidebar before removing your device from your Mac.

Delete any audiobooks that have been automatically synchronized to your device

Delete the audiobook from your Mac and sync your device to get rid of an undesirable audiobook.

Follow these steps to delete an audiobook from only your device while keeping it on your MacBook Air:

1. Connect your device to your MacBook Air 2022.
2. In the Finder 🔲 on your Mac, click **Audiobooks** in the button bar after choosing your device from the sidebar.
3. Uncheck the boxes next to the audiobooks you want to delete in the Audiobook list.

4. Synchronize your MacBook Air with your iPad and iPhone.

If you remove an item that syncs automatically from your Mac, it will no longer be available on your device when you next sync. Click the **Eject button** ⏏ in the Finder sidebar before removing your device from your MacBook Air.

Synchronize books between your MacBook Air and iPad or iPhone

You can sync all of your books from your Mac to your mobile or just a few of them.

Sync your books to your device:

1. Connect your device to your MacBook Air 2022.
2. Choose the device from the Finder sidebar in your Mac's Finder.
3. In the button bar, choose **Books**.
4. To enable book synchronization, check the "**Sync books onto [device name]**" option. By checking the option, synchronization is configured to send all your books to your device.

5. Choose the "**Selected books**" checkbox to sync a specific group of books.
6. Tick the boxes next to each book in the book list that you wish to sync. For any book, you don't want to sync, deselect the checkbox.
7. Click **Apply** when you're ready to sync.

Remove automatically synced books from your device

Delete the book from your Mac, then sync your device to get rid of any unwanted books. Follow these methods to delete a book from only your device while keeping it on your Mac:

1. Connect your device to your MacBook Air 2022.
2. In the Finder 🔍 on your Mac, click **Books** in the button bar after choosing your device from the sidebar.
3. In the list of books, uncheck the checkbox next to the title you wish to delete.
4. Connect your Mac to the device.

If you remove an item that syncs automatically from your Mac, it will no longer be available on your device when you next sync.

Synchronize images between your MacBook Air and iPad or iPhone

Photos on your Mac can be synced with your device. You can sync all or a specific subset of the photographs in your Mac's Photos library. You can also sync your favorite albums or individual person images, for instance. Additionally, you can sync pictures from your Pictures folder and other photo-specific folders. For instance, you may import pictures taken with a camera into a Finder folder. Your images will be organized in different folders inside of one another, and you can sync those folders to a device.

Note: Your photos are updated automatically if you currently use iCloud Photos on your Mac and other devices.

Synchronize images to your device:

1. Connect your device to your MacBook Air.
2. Choose the device from the Finder sidebar in your Mac's Finder.

3. Select **Pictures** from the button bar. When iCloud Photos is on, the Photos button in the button bar does not provide any photo syncing options.

4. Tick the box that says "**Sync Photos to your device from,**" then from the pop-up menu, choose Photos, Pictures, or a folder.

5. Choose one of the available options:
   - To sync photos from the Photos app, choose either "**Selected albums**" or "**All photos and albums**". Select the checkboxes next to the albums you want to sync in the Albums list by clicking the "**Selected albums**" button. To see your photos organized by that category, click **Photos or People**.
   - To sync photos from a folder, choose "**Selected folders**" or "**All folders.**" Select the tick boxes of the folders you want to sync in the Folders list if you choose "**Selected folders.**"

6. Pick any of the available synchronization options:
   - Tick the "**Add videos**" box when synchronizing from a folder or Photos library to add videos.

- To sync the photos you've marked as favorites, check the **"Only favorites"** option when synchronizing from the Photos app.
- To sync just photos taken within a certain period, check the **"Automatically add photos from" checkbox** when synchronizing from the Photos app.

7. Click **Apply** when you're ready to sync.

Remove automatically synced photos from your device

You can delete individual photos from the Photos app or a folder from your Mac, then sync your device to eliminate the undesired photos.

Follow these procedures to delete a picture album or folder from your Mac:

1. First, connect your device to your MacBook Air.
2. In the Finder on your Mac, click **Photos** in the button bar after choosing your device in the sidebar.
3. Uncheck the boxes next to the albums or folders you want to delete in the folders list.

4. Lastly, synchronize your MacBook Air with the device.

Synchronize files from your Mac to your iPad or iPhone

Files can be moved from your Mac to your device in the following steps:

1. Connect your device to your MacBook Air.
2. Choose the device from the Finder sidebar in your Mac's Finder.
3. In the button bar, choose **Files**. On your device, a list of the applications that enable file sharing will be displayed.
4. From a Finder window, drag a file or group of files onto the name of an app in the list. As soon as the files are uploaded, they are instantly accessible via the app on the device.
5. To see files that have already been transferred to your device, click the arrow $>$ next to the program name.

Select the files under the app's name, hit **Command-Delete**, and then click Delete to remove them. From there, the device promptly deletes the data. When transferring files in this manner, syncing is not necessary.

Chapter 4

How to Use and Customize the Dock

When it comes to personalization, the options available to you on your MacBook Air are almost limitless, regardless of the model you use. You can now install widgets in the Notification Center, download applications that were exclusive to the iPhone and iPad, and do a great deal more.

How to Customize the Dock on Your Mac

You have a lot of control over the Dock's settings, so you can customize it to seem more like your own. If you want to modify either its size or its position, you can do so using the System Preferences in the following manner:

The steps:

1. In the upper-left-hand corner of your display, click the **Apple** menu to open it on your MacBook Air.
2. Navigate to the **System Preferences menu**.
3. Choose **Dock & Menu Bar** from the menu.

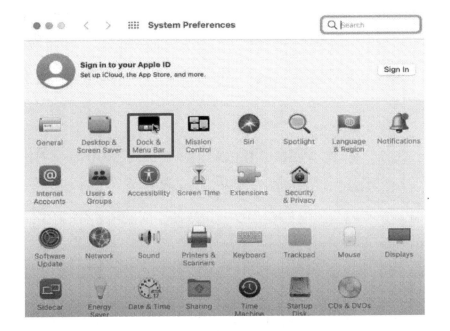

Resize the Dock

To make the most of the space on your screen, not only are you able to increase the size of the icons in the dock, but you can also adjust the actual size of the icons. There are two different approaches to doing this, the first is managed via the computer's System Preferences.

The steps:

1. Launch **System Preferences**.
2. Click **Dock & Menu Bar**.

3. In the Size section, use the slider to alter the size of the Dock until it matches your preferences.

The second approach of enlarging the Dock does not require you to launch any other applications at any point. However, a degree of accuracy is required to ensure that the pointer is positioned in the appropriate location at all times.

The steps:

1. Position your mouse above the vertical separator that separates the docked applications from the Downloads folder.
2. When the pointer changes into an arrow that points up and down, click and drag it toward the top of the screen.
3. Press the release button after you have achieved the Dock size you desire.

Add a Spacer to the Dock

When it comes to personalizing the Dock on macOS 12 Monterey, the option to add spacers is one of the best-hidden features that can be found.

You cannot create standard folders for the various kinds of programs, this makes it much simpler to arrange apps according to their categories or just to group them.

The steps:

1. Launch the **Terminal application** on your MacBook Air.
2. Type the following command:
   - defaults write com.apple.dock persistent-apps-
   - array-add '{"tile-type"="spacer-tile";}'; killall Dock
3. Select **Return**.

When you hit the **Return key**, the Dock will momentarily vanish, and any previously minimized applications will become visible on the screen. After the procedure is finished, there will be a void at the end of your dock to which you may move your items.

After that, you can move the spacer about any way you see fit, positioning it between other applications to create a cluster of them all at once.

Hide Recent Applications

After completing the preliminary steps of the setup procedure, the first thing that you should do is to "**declutter**" the Dock by removing any unnecessary items.

The steps:

1. Launch **System Preferences**.
2. Click **Dock & Menu Bar**.
3. Select the "**Show recent apps in Dock**" option and click the "**Check**" button.

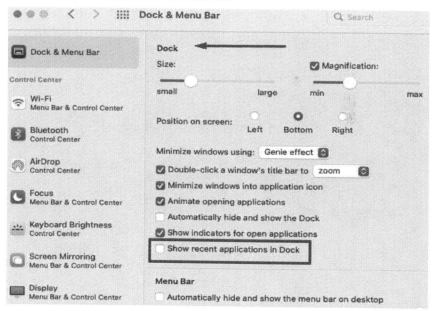

The additional part on the Dock will vanish as soon as the checkbox is selected, leaving you with just the programs that you want, the Downloads folder, and the **Trash Bin**.

Change Position of the Dock

For several years, users of macOS had to depend on commands entered into the Terminal to relocate the dock. Thankfully, those days are behind us since the location of the Dock can now be modified directly under **System Preferences**.

The steps:

1. Ensure you right-click on the divider between your downloads and apps.
2. Using your mouse pointer, highlight the position on the screen.
3. Choose an option from the following list:
   - Left
   - Bottom
   - Right

You can also modify the location of the dock by going into System Preferences and selecting the appropriate option:

1. On your MacBook Air, launch **System Preferences**.
2. Click **Dock & Menu Bar**.
3. Select one of the following options that will appear next to Position on screen:
   - Left
   - Bottom
   - Right

Moving the Dock to the left or right will cause you to lose some horizontal screen space, but it will increase the number of pages you can see simultaneously in the vertical direction.

Adjust Magnification

When it comes to the Dock in macOS Monetary, one useful feature is that you can choose to have the programs enlarged anytime your mouse is lingering over them. You will be able to reduce the size of the dock by doing so, but you will still be able to click and access the appropriate programs whenever you want them.

The steps:

1. Launch **System Preferences**.

2. Click **Dock & Menu Bar.**
3. Select the **"Magnification"** checkbox and click **the "Check" button.**
4. Make the necessary adjustments to the slider.

When you are making use of the Magnification feature on the Dock, you will want to make certain that the slider is moved to a position that is higher than that of the **"Size" option.** This makes the icons in the Dock larger when the cursor is moved over them in that area.

Add and Remove Apps from the Dock

When it comes to personalizing the Dock, one of the fundamental features is the ability to add or remove applications. When you do this, it guarantees that the only applications that appear are the ones that you use most often.

The steps:

1. Open Launchpad by clicking its icon in the Dock.
2. Find the application you wish to add to the Dock and click its icon.

3. Move the app to the position on the Dock that you want it to be in by dragging and dropping it there.

- Right-click on the application you want to keep in the Dock, choose **Options** from the drop-down menu and then select the **Keep in Dock option**.

If you want the Dock to seem more personal, you'll want to get rid of any applications you don't plan on using in the future. This is the procedure for removing applications from the Dock.

The steps:

1. Using Spotlight, search for the application that you wish to delete from the Dock.
2. Right-click the app.
3. Using your pointer, highlight the Options menu.
4. Select the "**Remove from Dock**" option.

If the application you want to remove from the Dock is already open, you can delete it by clicking and holding it, dragging it away from the Dock, and releasing it.

Add Folders to the Dock

The Downloads and Trash Can folders are already there in the Dock. However, it is also possible to add more folders to the dock.

The steps:

1. On your MacBook Air, launch the **Finder application** .
2. Go to the folder you want to add to the Dock, and click the **Add button**.
3. Select **Open Folder** from the context menu.
4. Select "**Add to Dock**" from the submenu of the drop-down menu.

Chapter 5

How to Set up & Edit iCloud

iCloud allows you to store information like pictures, passwords, videos and so much more to use later or in the future.

The steps:

1. Select **System Preferences** from the Apple menu.
2. Select **Apple ID**.
3. Enter your Apple ID username and password if you are not already logged in.
4. Choose **iCloud**.
5. A list of iCloud services will appear. Select them by checking the box next to them.

You shouldn't typically modify your iCloud account information. However, there are certain circumstances in which you may want to do this, such as when you want to alter the email address connected to your iCloud account. In the macOS iCloud preferences, you can modify your iCloud name, picture, contacts, security settings, devices, and payment information.

Change Your iCloud Account Information

The steps:

1. Click **"Apple ID"** under **"Apple** [image: Apple logo] menu > System Preferences."** You will also find these options on the pane's left side:
   - Overview
   - Name, Phone, and Email
   - Security & Password
   - Shipping & Payment.

1. Overview

An overview is only a summary of what the options are.

2. Name, Phone, Email

You can change your name, birthdate, email address, and phone number by selecting Name, Phone, and Email from the menu.

Enable or disable the following:

- **Announcements:** This enables you to get (or not) notifications, suggestions, and updates on Apple goods, services, and software.
- **Apple, Music, TV, and Others:** By doing this, you will get suggestions from Apple for apps, music, movies, TV shows, books, podcasts, Apple Pay, Apple Card, and other products, as well as new releases, exclusive content, special deals, and recommendations.
- **Apple Newsletter:** This enables you to get Apple suggestions.

3. Security & Password

You can update your password and activate or disable two-factor authentication by selecting the **Password & Security option**. Additionally, if you sign in using a different device or web browser, you can modify your list of trusted phone numbers that are used to confirm your identification. To sign in on another device or at iCloud.com, you can request a verification code to be sent to your phone.

Also, you have the option to enable or disable the **Recovery Key function**. When you create one, the only method to reset your password is to login in with your Apple ID on another device or, if or when you set one up, by entering your recovery key. You can change the list of websites and applications that allow you to sign in using your Apple ID.

4. Shipping and payment

Choose the payment method you want to use to make purchases or sign up for services from Apple by selecting the **Payment & Shipping option**. The Payment & Shipping option will display your cash balance and card balance if you decide to set up an Apple Card.

Access your iCloud content on your MacBook Air 2022

Your most crucial data, including files, images, and more, is kept secure, current, and accessible across all of your devices with the aid of iCloud. Every Apple device is linked to an iCloud storage, with default 5 GB storage. Your available space is not affected by purchases you make from the iTunes Store, Apple Books, Apple TV app, or App Store.

If you want additional storage or premium services like HomeKit Secure Video compatibility, Hide My

Email, Custom email domains, and iCloud Private Relay (beta), you should subscribe to iCloud+.

iCloud Drive will automatically save your desktop and Documents folder:

Save files to your desktop or Documents folder, and they will be instantly made available on iCloud Drive so you can view them from anywhere. You can access files on your MacBook Air, your iPhone or iPad in the Files app, the web at iCloud.com, or a Windows PC in the iCloud for Windows app while using iCloud Drive. Anywhere you access the file, your adjustments will be visible when you make changes to it on a device or in iCloud Drive.

- To begin, open **System Preferences**, choose **Apple ID** and then select iCloud.
- Select "**Desktop & Documents Folders**" under Options after choosing **iCloud Drive**.

With iCloud Photos and Shared Albums, you can save and share photos:

Store your photo library in iCloud to access your pictures, movies, and modifications across all of your devices. You can share your images and videos with selected individuals and allow them to share their photos, videos, and comments.

- To begin, open **System Preferences**, and pick Apple ID, iCloud, and Photos.

Use Find My Mac to locate your MacBook Air:

If you have **Find My Mac** enabled, you can use it to find your lost MacBook Air on a map, lock its screen, and even remotely delete its data.

- Open **System Preferences**, click **Apple ID**, click **iCloud**, and then choose **Find My Mac** to enable **Find My Mac**. Take note that only one user account on your MacBook Air can have **Find My Mac** enabled.

Get more using iCloud+:

Get out of the storage limits and sharing options of iCloud with the subscription service iCloud+, along with extra capabilities. Through Family Sharing, you can share any iCloud+ storage plan size. Additionally, iCloud Private Relay (beta), HomeKit Secure Video, and personalized email domains for your iCloud.com Mail address are all included with iCloud+.

What you get with an iCloud+ membership is as follows:

- **Storage**: iCloud storage options of 50 GB, 200 GB, or 2 TB.
- **iCloud Private Relay (beta)**: Private Relay is a service that safeguards your unencrypted communication and masks your IP address in Safari. You can surf the web more privately and securely when it is turned on.
- **Hide My Email**: Send and receive emails without disclosing your email address by creating one-of-a-kind, arbitrary email addresses that forward to your inbox.
- Connect your home security cameras with the Home App to record video and access it from anywhere. All of the videos are end-to-end encrypted, and none of it uses up any of your iCloud storage.
- **Custom email domains**: Add a unique domain name to your iCloud Mail account. Your family members' iCloud Mail accounts might be invited to use the same domain.
- **Family Sharing**: Each iCloud+ plan can be shared with up to five family members, allowing

everyone to make use of the additional storage and features with just one subscription.

How to Sign Out of iCloud on your MacBook Air

Follow these procedures to log out of your iCloud account:

1. In the top-left corner of the screen, click the Apple ⬛ Menu.
2. Click **Apple ID** in the top-right corner of **System Preferences**.
3. Select **Overview** in the left-hand panel, then **click Sign Out** at the bottom.
4. Before you log out, you could be prompted to retain a backup of your iCloud data. If you wish to make a copy of it, click **Keep a Copy**. This implies that data from iCloud's services will continue to be accessible on your Mac even after you log out of iCloud. Choose **Save a Copy** after selecting the data you wish to keep. If you want to store the data just on the iCloud's server and erase it from your Mac, you should select **None**.

5. To continue, you will be prompted to enter your Apple ID password if **Find My Mac** is activated.

6. To complete signing out, you could be prompted for your Mac's password. You may then securely log out of your iCloud account on your Mac.

Private Relay

For iCloud+ users, Private Relay is a new privacy function. You can use the function if you pay for iCloud storage at the 50GB tier or above.

Setting up iCloud Private Relay

The steps:

1. Open **System Preferences** in the Applemenu on your Mac, choose **Apple ID**, and then pick **iCloud** from the sidebar.

2. Select **Options** after selecting **Private Relay**. To upgrade to a storage plan that includes iCloud+, click the **Upgrade button** if it shows up.

3. Enter your Apple ID password if prompted, then click **Continue**.

4. Select any of the following:
   - To enable or disable Private Relay, choose the **Turn On or Turn Off option**.
   - **Choose an IP Address Location:** Click **Maintain General Location** to keep your general IP address location as it was initially. Click **Use Nation and Time Zone** to use a wider IP address location in your country and time zone.

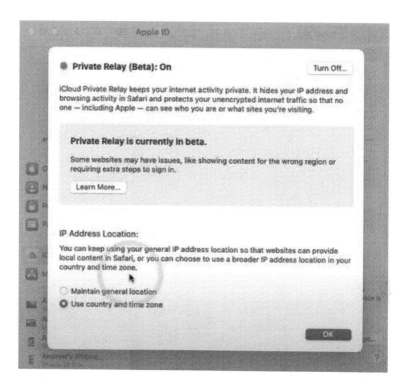

5. Press **OK**.

Turn iCloud Private Relay on or off on your Ethernet or Wi-Fi network

Your Wi-Fi and Ethernet network options are adjusted to restrict IP address tracking when you sign up for iCloud+ and enable iCloud Private Relay (beta). The network option can be enabled or disabled. Note that iCloud Private Relay might not operate on all networks.

The steps:

1. Open **System Preferences** from the Apple menu on your Mac, choose **Network**, and then pick your **Wi-Fi or Ethernet connection** from the sidebar.
2. Select or uncheck the Limit IP Address Tracking option to enable or disable **iCloud Private Relay**.

Chapter 6

Set Up and Use Screen Time on Your Mac

Check how much time you and your children spend on apps, websites, and other online activities with Screen Time. Turn on Screen Time on your Mac-Book Air 2022 to see how much time you spend using it and other devices. You can examine statistics that indicate app usage, the number of alerts you get, and how often you use your devices when Screen Time is enabled.

How to Set Up Mac Screen Time

You can activate Screen Time by going to the **System Preferences** pane on your Mac, provided it is running the most recent version of macOS 12 Monterey.

The steps:

1. Select **System Preferences** from the Apple menu.
2. Choose **Screen Time** .
3. In the lower-left corner, click **Options**.
4. Then select **Turn On**.

5. Choose "**Share across devices**" to see user data for every other device connected to iCloud with your Apple ID. Go to **Settings > Screen Time**⌛ on each iPhone, iPad, or iPod touch, then enable the same option.

You can enable Screen Time directly from your kid's devices if you're using Family Sharing to manage a child's account.

Use your MacBook Air also to carry this function below:

1. Select **System Preferences** from the Apple menu, then select **Family Sharing**.
2. Select your child's name from the list on the right after clicking **Screen Time** in the sidebar.
3. To reaccess the Screen Time settings, click the **Open Screen Time icon**.
4. Select your kid's name from the menu in the top-left corner.
5. In the lower-left corner, click **Options**.
6. Finally, select **Turn On**.

To change an administrator account into an ordinary user account after adding a Screen Time passcode, choose **Don't allow this user to manage this account**.

How to Monitor App Usage

- By choosing the **App Use side tab** after setting Screen Time, you can begin seeing your app usage statistics as bar charts. Go through your Screen Time history by using the arrow buttons in the top-right corner of the screen, where each bar represents a day.
- You can also choose a bar to get usage statistics broken down by category (Social, Games, Productivity & Finance, etc.). Additionally, monitor use time by program or category by switching between the Apps and Categories tabs.
- The app use statistics would also include your activities on other Apple devices if you had previously chosen the Share across devices option. Check the pull-down option at the bottom of the screen for use statistics broken down by device.
- Access the Alerts side bar in addition to the App Usage section to see the total number of notifications you've received from each app. To filter stats by the device once again, use the device selection option.

- If you want to calculate how often you've used each Apple device's app, choose the **Pickups side menu**.

How to Place App Limits

You can start setting time limitations for app categories or specific applications if your Screen Time uses statistics to show that you're using your Mac for an excessive amount of time. Additionally, you can make your groups that include different applications and categories by following the steps below:

1. Open the Screen Time side tab for App Limits.
2. To start setting a new app limit, click the **Plus + symbol**.
3. Choose an app category. Expand the categories and choose the applications you want to include by checking the boxes next to them. This will allow you to set time limitations for individual apps.
4. Define a time frame; it should, by default, include all seven days of the week. If you want to stop your kid from exceeding the time restriction, use the "Block" at the end of the limit option (available only if you've set up a Screen Time

password). If you want to make a custom schedule, use the radio option next to "Custom."

5. To save your changes, click **Done**.

Once the time restriction has expired, your MacBook Air will automatically prevent you from using any programs in a category or custom group. You have the option to disregard the restriction; therefore, self-control is essential.

The Time Limit overlay will include an **Ask For Extra Time** option if you've established app limitations for a kid, which they may use to request more time from you. Additionally, you can change, deactivate, or eliminate app limits whenever you want by going to the App Restrictions section of Screen Time.

Note that app restrictions apply to all of your Apple devices. If you set a time restriction for using Safari, running the program on an iPhone will reduce the time you have available to use it on your MacBook Air 2022.

How to Set Downtime on Your MacBook Air

Be compelled to stop using your Mac (and other Apple devices) at a specific time of the day using a downtime schedule in addition to app limitations. You are only permitted to use the applications that are authorized during that time (more on that next). You can opt to set up Downtime as a custom schedule or every day of the week by switching to the Downtime side menu and selecting **Turn On**.

How to Continually Allow Apps

You will need unlimited access to at least a few necessary applications, regardless of app restrictions or a shutdown schedule. For instance, you could wish to continue using Messages at any hour of the day.

- Select the **Always Allowed option** and tick the boxes next to each app you want to be exempt from the Screen Time limitations to sort that out.

Setting Communication Limits

You can also set communication restrictions for applications like FaceTime and Messages through the Communication side menu in Screen Time for Mac.

- Select **Contacts Only or Contacts & Groups** with at Least One Contact under the **During screen time** area as necessary to restrict one-on-one and group interactions.

- Additionally, you can limit idle chat to just certain contacts. Select **Specific Contacts** from the **During downtime** section by clicking the **Edit button**.

How to Manage Privacy & Content

Parents are allowed to choose from a wide range of content control choices offered by Screen Time. To navigate between the Content, Stores, Apps, and other areas choose **the Content & Privacy side tab**. You have the option to restrict adult websites, graphic literature and music, and Game Center private chat, among other things. However, some limitations will only apply to iOS and iPadOS devices.

Chapter 7

How to Setup Family Sharing

You can set up Apple's Family Sharing function on your Mac. The program enables you to lend family members access to your books, videos, and other media and apps you have personally bought.

How to Set Up Family Sharing

The steps:

1. On your MacBook Air, click the **Apple icon tab** in the top-left corner of the desktop to access System Preferences. Family Sharing should appear if your Apple ID account is active on your Mac. If you can't see the icon to return to System Preferences, just sign in with your Apple ID.
2. Click **Family Sharing**. You will be prompted in this box whether you wish to manage the family's schedule. To confirm, click the **Next button**. You'll also be prompted whether you want to share your purchases in the next window. Simply

choose to use a different account as well and select **Next**.

3. Your payment information associated with your Apple ID account will be shown in the payment window. Additionally, an option underneath **Next** that lets you choose a different payment method is available. Your card will be used to make any purchases made by the family members you add to the program. Choose **Next**. Click **Agree** if you accept the terms and conditions.

4. Family Sharing on a Mac enables you to share the location of your connected devices with family members in addition to sharing applications and other content. Select "**Done**."

5. At this point, you can now add users to Family Sharing on your Mac. Then enter their name or email address by clicking the **Add Family Member button** and choosing **Continue**. To continue, you must confirm your Apple ID password and specific information on the payment card associated with your account.

6. Click the **Plus + button** and repeat the previous instructions to include new people in the group.

Add Family Members to a Family Sharing Group

The family organizer can add up to five family members to the Family Sharing group. Everyone in the family is given a request to attend the gathering.

The steps:

1. From the Apple menu on your Mac, pick **System Preferences**, then Family Sharing from the sidebar.
2. Select one of the following actions after clicking the Add button ✛:
   - To invite family members, click **Invite People** and then adhere to the prompts on the screen. You can also choose to Invite **in Person** and request that the invitee input their Apple ID and password on your Mac if they are close by. If not, you may use AirDrop, Messages, or Mail to send the invitation. The person you're inviting must first create an Apple ID to accept your invitation if they don't already have one.

- **Create an Apple ID for a kid:** Then adhere to the on-screen steps after selecting **Create Child Account**.
- After new family members confirm the Apple ID they use to share iTunes Store, App Store, and Apple Books purchases, the family has access to the purchases they make. In the Family Sharing options, any family member can make this choice.

As the family's coordinator or organizer, you can resend an email invitation to a recipient who hasn't yet accepted it. Click **Family** under the Family Sharing options, then click **Resend Invitation** next to the relative's name.

Change the Credit Card Shared by a Family Sharing Group

The family organizer can change the shared credit card used by every family member in your Family Sharing group by following the steps below:

1. From the Apple menu on your Mac, pick **System Preferences**, then click **Family Sharing**.
2. Next, click **Purchase Sharing** from the sidebar.

3. To manage your payment methods in the App Store, click the **Edit button** next to **Shared Payment Method** and then adhere to the onscreen instructions.

Remove Family Members from a Family Sharing Group

You can remove family members from the Family Sharing group as the family organizer. A person can join or create a new family group after you remove them from the current one. Each individual, however, is only permitted to join two family groupings each year. (Re-joining or starting a new family group counts against this restriction.) You can't take away a child under 13 from a family group (age varies by country or region).

Here's how:

1. From the Apple menu on your Mac, pick **System Preferences**, then **Family Sharing** from the sidebar.
2. After selecting the family member, click **Remove [family member]**, and click **OK**.

3. The individual you kick out of the family retains the things or items they bought with the family credit card, but they instantly lose access to other things.

- In the Purchased area of the iTunes Store, App Store, and Apple Books, things belonging to other family members are no longer visible.
- If someone else buys the family member's previously downloaded DRM-protected music, movies, TV programs, books, and applications, they are no longer functional. DRM-protected material that was downloaded from the former family member's library is no longer accessible to other family members.
- If a family member made in-app purchases using an app that someone else initially bought, those purchases are no longer accessible.
- When a family member uses the **Find My** app on a Mac, on iCloud.com, or an iOS or iPadOS device, the whereabouts of other family members' devices do not show up.

Change the Services Family Members Use in Family Sharing

Add, modify, or discontinue the services your Family Sharing group's members may use.

The steps:

1. On your Mac, choose **Family Sharing** 🔗 under the **Apple menu** > **System Preferences**.
2. From there, carry out the following:
   - **Purchase Sharing**: To activate or disable purchase sharing for your family, modify your payment method, or alter other options, choose **Purchase Sharing** in the sidebar.
   - **iCloud Storage**: From the sidebar, choose **iCloud Storage**. Next, choose whether to share your current 200GB or 2TB iCloud Storage plan with others or to upgrade to a Family-shareable plan. Family members can also keep individual storage plans if they so wish. Family members have a grace period to use the shared iCloud storage after you cease sharing it, after which they must buy their storage plan.

- **Location Sharing:** In the sidebar, click **Location Sharing**. Then, check or uncheck the boxes next to the family members you wish to share your location with.

- **Screen Usage:** To obtain weekly data on kids' screen time and set limits for what you want to regulate, choose **Screen Time** in the sidebar and it will open the **Screen Time settings**.

- **Ask To Buy:** Click on the sidebar option, then check or uncheck the box next to family members.

- **Family Sharing subscriptions:** You can let family members use your Apple Music, TV channel, and other subscriptions. This option also allows you to see shared subscriptions in the Family Sharing sidebar.

- **Apple Music:** To examine your family's subscription status, choose **Apple Music** from the sidebar. When one family member subscribes, all other family members do so automatically.

- **Apple TV:** To monitor the status of your family's subscription, choose **Apple TV** in the sidebar. When one family member subscribes, all other family members do so automatically.

- **Apple Arcade:** Click **Apple Arcade** in the sidebar to check your family's subscription status (not accessible in all nations or regions). When one family member subscribes, all other family members do so automatically.
- **Apple News:** To monitor your family's subscription status, choose **Apple News+** in the sidebar.

Share Purchase with Others in Your Family Sharing Group

Get quick access to purchases shared by other group members. Their purchases are always available for download on your Mac, iOS, and iPadOS devices.

Your purchases are similarly accessible to other group members. Individual purchases that you don't want other group members to see may be hidden.

Download and View Purchases Made by Other Family Members

- Using the Songs app, log in, then choose **Account > Family Purchases** to see or download music. After selecting a family member, download the desired things.

- Using the App Store app 🅰, log in, then choose **Store > View My Account** to view or download applications.
- Using the Books app 📖, log in, then choose **Account > View My Account** to view or download books. After selecting a family member, download the desired items you want.

A family member's purchase is invoiced straight to the family organizer's account when they start it. When an item is bought, it is shared with the rest of the family and added to the account of the person who initiated the transaction. Each participant retains the products they bought, even if the family organizer paid for them if the family organizer ever decides to end Family Sharing.

Hide a Purchase from Other Family Members

You can make your purchases from the iTunes Store, the App Store, and Apple Books inaccessible to other family members by following the steps below.

1. To hide songs, log in to the **Music app**, go to **Account > Family Purchases**, and then click **Hide**. Place the cursor over the item you wish to hide, select the kind of content you wish to hide, click the **Delete button** ⊗, and then choose **Hide**.

2. Using the App Store app, sign in, then select **Store > View My Account** to hide applications. Put the cursor over the app you wish to hide, choose **Hide Purchase** from the **More Options menu** ⋯, and then click **Hide Purchase**.

3. To hide books, log in to the Books app, navigate to **Account > View My Account**, and then click **Hide Books**. Put the cursor over the book you wish to hide, then select it, select **Remove**, and then select **Hide item** from the More Options menu ⋯.

Make Hidden Items Visible to other Family Members

You may wish to make your individual Apple Books, Music, and App Store purchases visible to your family members.

The steps:

1. To stop songs from being hidden, sign in to the Music app and navigate to **Account > Family Purchases**. To unhide an item, scroll to **Hidden Purchases**, click **Manage**, and then click on **Unhide**.

2. To stop applications from being hidden, sign in to the **App Store app** and choose **Store > View My Account**. Click **Manage**, and then click **Unhide** for the item under the section "**Hidden Items**."

3. To stop books from being hidden, log in to the **Books app**, then choose **Account > View My Account**. Then click Unhide for the item after selecting **Manage Hidden Purchases**.

Stop Sharing Your Purchases

Your family members lose access to all shared iTunes Store, Apple Books, and App Store purchases when you cease sharing your purchases, and they are unable to make new shared purchases.

The steps:

1. From the Apple menu on your Mac, pick **System Preferences**, then click on **Family Sharing**. Next, click **Purchase Sharing** from the sidebar.
2. In the Account details section, uncheck **Share My Purchases**.

Chapter 8

How to Enable Focus Mode

Use **Focus** when you need to avoid distractions and remain on track. While using **Focus**, you can stop and quiet all alerts or selectively enable certain notifications, such as those from coworkers on a pressing project. To let people know you're busy, you may also let them know that you've turned off your alerts.

Setting up Focus Mode

The steps:

1. Select **Focus** under Settings.
2. At the top of the screen, click the **Focus tab**.

3. Select an existing Focus Mode from the list that is shown.

4. To add a new one, click on the **+ sign** in the upper right corner.

5. Select "**Custom**" or one of the recommended Focus Modes, such as "**Gaming.**"

6. Select your Focus Mode, then press **Return**.

7. Also, select a color.

8. Next, if desired, choose an icon.

9. Click **Next**. From there, you can set who can distract you and which applications are allowed to interrupt you.

How to Set Up Details of Your Focus Mode

Every new Focus Mode you build has its controls in addition to the main, overall choices. That comes in three pieces on the Mac.

- The first consideration is from whom or what you will accept alerts. For times when the mail has to be delivered, you can put any app you like here, or you could name someone.

- There is no option to choose a person's mobile, workplace, or home number, unlike most other features of macOS 12 Monterey. You cannot choose whether to accept calls, Face-Time, messages, or both.

- There are only some individuals important enough to you to wish to hear from at any time, or if at all, they attempt to contact you.
- The next feature is the ability to automate Focus Mode's activation at a specific setting. You have three options below:
  - Time-based Focus Mode
  - Location-based
  - App-based

The time-based option most closely looks like **Do Not Disturb nighttime mode.** On Monday through Friday, you can set it to turn on automatically at 7:00 and turn it off again at 18:00.

Even if you don't keep regular hours, you probably spend the weekdays at the same workplace. Location-based allows you to set it up such that a particular Focus Mode activates as you approach the location and turns off when you leave that location.

From the control center

There is a simple ON switch in addition to all the automatic methods of activating precise Focus Modes to suit your task.

The steps:

1. Open **Control Center** on the Mac.
2. Select a Focus.
3. Select **Do Not Disturb** or one of the Focus Modes from the list.
4. You can choose how long you want it to run for.

How to Activate Automatic Responses

The steps:

1. Select **Notifications in System Preferences** on your MacBook Air 2022.
2. At the top of the screen, click the **Focus tab**.
3. Click **Turn on auto-reply**.

Since you have chosen one of your Focus Modes, you are unable to view that choice. At the bottom of the list of focus modes, select **Options** to return to viewing these default settings.

Control Notifications

- In the left-hand column, choose the new Focus mode. Select **Plus + under "Allowed Notifications From."** To give someone permission to contact you, choose them from your contacts list and click **Add**. To do the same for applications, click the **Apps tab** under Allowed Notifications. This will let some Mac programs give you alerts while disabling all others.

- Click **Options** next to **Allowed Notifications From**. Here, you can choose which contacts to accept calls from (such as your favorites or all contacts) and whether to accept repeated calls. Finally, yet importantly, you can instruct your Mac to accept time-sensitive alerts even while Focus mode is on. This implies that, for example, you can still get notifications about a calendar event that is about to begin.

How to Automatically Run Focus Mode

- Turn on the toggle at the top of the Focus tab in **System Preferences** to manually activate the chosen Focus setting. When this occurs, you'll see an icon for Focus mode in your Mac's menu bar.

- You can change the Focus mode or manually specify whether it should run for an hour or later in the day. You can also manually activate one of your Focus modes using the Focus option in the Control Center.

- Program your Focus mode to begin automatically if you want a more hands-off approach. Click the **Plus + button** next to **Turn On Automatically**, then choose **Add Time Based Automation**. Select the days and hours when the Focus mode is in use.

- Additionally, you can program location-based automation to turn on Focus mode as soon as you reach a certain spot.

Other Focus Mode Options

To sync everything to other devices using the same Apple ID, make sure the **Share Across Devices** option in the bottom left corner is selected. Alternatively, make sure this box is unticked if, for example, you solely use your Mac for business and don't want your Work Focus mode to influence your personal iPhone.

Your Mac will immediately notify anybody attempting to contact you while Focus mode is on that you are not accessible. Enable **Share Focus Status** under the Focus tab in System Preferences. This will create the impression that you are busy while also giving them the chance to call you if anything is very urgent.

Add or Remove a Focus

The steps:

1. On your MacBook Air 2022, choose **Notifications & Focus** under the **Apple menu** 🍎 > **System Preferences**.

2. Select **Focus** 🔔 and take any of the following actions:
   - **Adding a pre-existing Focus:** Select a Focus, such as "Gaming" or "Work," by clicking the **Add button** + at the bottom of the Focus list.
   - To create a unique Focus, choose **Custom** from the Focus list's Add button + at the

bottom. Click Add after entering a name and choosing an icon and color.

- A custom Focus can be modified by selecting it from the list and then clicking **Edit** at the bottom of the Focus list. Click **Done** after changing the name, color, or icon.
- To delete a focus, first choose it from the list and then click the **Remove** button — at the bottom of the focus list.

Chapter 9

How to use Quick Notes on a Mac

Despite not always functioning as expected, the new Quick Notes feature in macOS 12 Monterey is another improvement.

What Quick Note provides

- Quick note-taking of phone numbers
- A technique to bookmark a webpage so you can go back to it later.
- Tools for gathering website links
- The ability to pull up a note immediately and add to it.
- Your Apple devices are all synchronized with your notes.

These essentially consist of making, editing, and maintaining notes. Although there are tools in Quick Notes for each of these, they are not all equally effective or maybe equally polished.

How to Create Quick Notes

There are three methods for creating Quick Notes. Naturally, each has benefits, but they also have peculiarities.

Create Quick Notes with a Click

The first thing you will likely notice while using Quick Notes is a large white box that momentarily appears in the bottom right corner of your screen.

- You will have accidentally triggered what Apple refers to as Hot Corners by moving your mouse a bit too near to that area of the screen. Unless you've previously configured the Mac to do anything, like launch your screensaver, it will now launch Quick Notes when you move your cursor to the bottom right hot corner.
- Or, to be more precise, it will summon this enormous white box. Though it seems to be a note, it is not. It is a button, and pressing it activates a bigger button with controls for adding a new note.

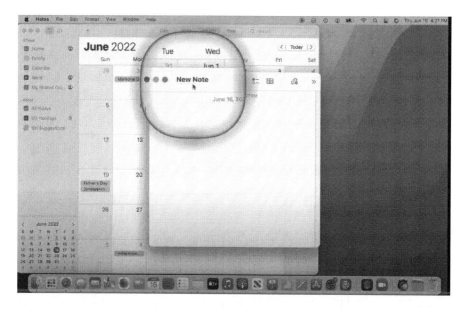

When you click on the white box that appears, the real Quick Note opens. Then, you have a lot of options, including:

- Just type a message.
- Add text or a picture.
- An app link (with limitations)
- Share the note with other people.
- Add to a current note (in certain circumstances)

You can create a link to the current Safari page by selecting the Link button, which creates a note with a link in it. You can also click that link afterward to return directly to the website in Safari.

Create Quick Notes by Selecting Text

This only works on Safari. You'll want the functionality to be system-wide despite how great it is in the browser now. However, you can now highlight part or all of the text on a page with Safari and right-click to display a menu. Select **Add to Quick Note or New Quick Note**.

It seems impossible to specify which earlier Quick Note you want to add to. It's either the latest or the last project you worked on. Quick Notes opens your most recent note by default, but you can modify this option in the Apple Notes app's Preferences. However, if you do, both New Quick Note and Add to Quick Note may end up performing the same action.

Create Quick Notes with a Keystroke

- By tapping a few keys on your keyboard, you can open a new Quick Note. Unfortunately, **Function-Q** should be the key you select.
- Standard Apple Magic Keyboards lack a Function key. Function keys come in multiples, but there is no Fn modifier as there is for Shift, Command, or Option.

- Select **Mission Control** under Keyboard, Short-cuts, and System Preferences. There will be a Quick Note option at the bottom of the list that displays on the right.

Adding and Editing to Quick Notes

Return to the Safari web page from which you wrote a Quick Note. Now you see why Apple displays a large white square in the bottom left: it allows it to display more information.

- When you return to that page, a Quick Note with a thumbnail of the previously stored note displays. Avoid clicking in the bottom right corner of the screen since doing so only creates a new, empty white square.
- Instead, click on the web page and the accompanying Quick Note will show up if you can't see it.

Add Links in Notes

To launch web pages and other applications quickly, you can add links to your notes.

Add URL Links:

1. Click a note in the notes list or double-click a note in the gallery view in the Notes program on your Mac, then choose **Edit > Substitutions > Smart Links** (a checkbox indicates it is enabled).

2. Choose one of these:
   - When you enter a URL, a link is created automatically.
   - To make text into a link, select the text, choose **Edit > Add Link**, and then enter or paste the URL.
   - Control-click the link, then choose an option to modify, delete, or open it.

Add Links to an App

You can provide a link to the content in compatible applications, like a podcast episode in Podcasts, a website in Safari, or a book in Books.

The steps:

1. Verify that the application you want to connect to is open and running. Open a website in Safari, for instance, or begin a podcast episode.

2. Open a note in the Notes app ▢ on your Mac, and then choose the **Link button** ⬡ in the toolbar.
3. Select **Add Link**.

When you return to the linked content in the app after adding a link to a Quick Note, a thumbnail of the Quick Note shows up in the corner of the screen.

Attach Files, Photos, and More in Notes

You may add map coordinates and webpage previews to enhanced iCloud notes and notes on your Mac. (If you are using an account other than iCloud or haven't updated your iCloud notes, you can still add map or web page URLs but won't see previews.) You can add documents like audio files, films, and images to your notes.

You cannot attach any files, map coordinates, or webpage previews to notes stored in an Exchange account.

Add images and files to notes:

1. Click a note in the notes list or double-click a note in the gallery view in the Notes program on your MacBook Air. Before you can attach anything to a locked note, it must first be unlocked.

2. Select one of the actions below to add an attachment:

   - Drag a file into the note from the desktop.
   - **Directly from your Photos library**: Drag a picture into the memo from your Photos library. Alternatively, drag a picture from the window that displays after clicking Photos on the Media toolbar button ∨ in Notes.
   - **Directly from the camera on your iPhone or iPad**: To take a photo or scan a document with your iPhone or iPad and insert it into your note, click at the start of a line, choose **File > Insert** from iPhone or iPad, and then select **Take Photo or Scan Documents**.
   - **Straight from your iPhone or iPad**: Click at the start of a line, choose **File > Insert from iPhone or iPad**, and then select **Add Drawing** to add a sketch that you've drawn on your iPad with your finger or an Apple Pencil to your note.

- Control-click a picture, scanned page, or PDF file and choose **View as Large Images or View as Small Images** to alter the size at which it appears in the note.

Add Items Directly from another App to a Note

A note can have an object attached to it from another app, such as a map location or a webpage preview. The attachment can be included in a new message or added to an already-existing letter.

The steps:

1. Perform any of the following actions from another app (such as Maps, Safari, Preview, or Photos):
   - To share from the toolbar, choose **Notes** by clicking the **Share icon** ⬆. Note that not all applications have the Share option.
   - **Share from a selection:** Control-click on some text or photos, then pick **Share > Notes**.
2. To add a new note, click **Save**.

Click the **Choose Note pop-up menu**, pick the note's name, and then click **Save** to add an attachment to an existing note.

View Attachments from All Your Notes

It is simple to explore attachments and discover the one you're looking for since you can examine attachments from your notes in a single window. Only notes saved on your Mac or upgraded iCloud accounts can have attachments visible.

The steps:

1. Select **View > Show Attachments Browser** from the Mac Notes app. A button for the attachments browser can be added to the toolbar for easy access.
2. Then select any of the below options:
   - **View attachments:** To view various attachment types, click a category button (such as Photos & Videos, Scans, or Maps). Pick **View > Hide Attachments Browser** to get back to the notes list. Even after entering your password to open your notes, please be aware that this view does not display attachments in locked notes.

- **Preview an attachment:** Press the **Spacebar** after selecting the attachment.
- **Look at the message that contains the attachment:** Select the attachment and select **View > Show in Note** from the menu.
- **Launch the attachment's default app:** Click the attachment twice.
- **Save a file attachment:** Select **Save Attachment** from the pop up when you control-click on the attachment. Maps and webpage previews are examples of attachments that cannot be saved using this approach.
- **Change an attachment's name:** Rename the attachment by selecting it with the control button, and then entering a new name.
- **Send the attachment to a different app:** To choose an app, control-click the attachment, then select **Share**.

After you attach photos (including scanned documents) and PDF documents to a note, you can annotate them.

Hot Corners

One of the most significant productivity enhancers on a Mac computer is a feature known as **Hot Corners**. Although this helpful function is tucked away in **System Preferences**, if you know where to search, it is simple to find and simple to set up.

Using **Hot Corners** on a Mac makes it simpler to browse by removing the need to memorize keyboard shortcuts. This can even speed up drag-and-drop activities. A few pointers can make utilizing Hot Corners effortless if you're acquainted with them and have developed the necessary memory. The function can be a little perplexing in certain situations.

What is Mac Hot Corners?

The phrase "Hot Corners" on a Mac denotes a particular event that takes place when moving the pointer into a screen corner. There are four Hot Corners, each of which has ten possible actions and the option to be disabled.

- Simply sliding the cursor to a corner on a MacBook trackpad or Mac mouse will open

Launchpad, create a **Quick Note**, turn the display off, and more.

Setting up Hot Corners

The steps:

1. Open **System Preferences**, pick **Screen Saver** from the **Desktop & Screen Saver pane**, click the **Screen Saver button** in the lower-right, and then click the "**Hot Corners**" **option** to activate Hot Corners. Four menus with hyphens encircling a little Mac display next to each corner if Hot Corners are deactivated. The currently chosen actions will be shown next to the corner that triggers them if any Hot Corners have previously been designated.

2. To see a list of options, choose one of **macOS'** **Hot Corner menus**. Mission Control, which displays all open programs, Application Windows, which displays the current app's windows, the Notification Center, or the Desktop can all be configured to open from any corner.

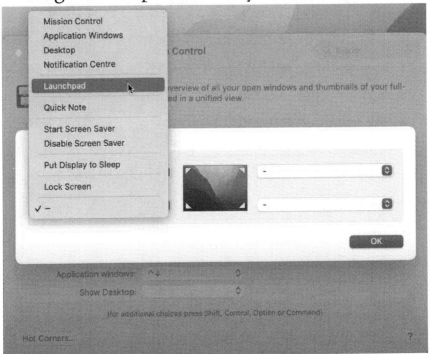

3. Mac's Hot Corner can be configured to manage the screen saver, enabling you to read while it's on without having to wait for it to turn on or off. You could decide to immediately lock the screen of your Mac with a Hot Corner or put the display to sleep.

How to use the Hot Corners in macOS 12 Monterey

By moving the cursor towards a diagonal corner, you can do any of the tasks linked to a Hot Corner. Since getting near is insufficient, there is no need to worry about this obstructing typical usage. To initiate the action, you must fully press into the top-left, top-right, bottom-left, or bottom-right corners.

Use macOS Hot Corners for Easy Drag and Drop

- When dragging text, files, or photos to another window, you can use Hot Corners. If you often have several overlapping windows open, this saves significant time and work. You can use Hot Corners rather than rearranging the screen to put the source and destination next to one other in a split screen. This greatly enhances the drag-and-drop functionality in macOS.
- Dragging to a Hot Corner that is configured to the Desktop, Mission Control, or Application Windows displays those areas as a drop zone.

What if the Hot Corners don't work?

Hot Corners on your MacBook Air 2022 might not always function as intended. Most often, this is due to the connection and configuration of one or more additional monitors as an extended display.

In this configuration, some Hot Corners may be seen on the secondary monitor since MacOS interprets the two panels as one giant display. For instance, the left Hot Corners could operate properly, but if you go to the right corner or edge, the pointer will show up on the second screen's expanded version. Resetting the power management system is required to solve the issue.

Here's how to fix both problems.

The steps:

1. Launch **macOS' System Preferences** and go to the **Displays tab**. Adjust the secondary display's position so that it is not perfectly aligned with the main display. You can use a Hot Corner on both the primary and secondary screens if the main screen corner overlaps a corner of the other display. The disadvantage is that macOS 12 Monterey

may misinterpret the physical placement of the additional display. This implies that rather than transferring smoothly, the pointer will hop as you move it to the other display.

2. Reset the system management controller (SMC), which governs your Mac's power, if multiple displays are not the issue. Hot Corners are connected to Screen Saver and Sleep, so the SMC might prevent this feature from working normally. To reset the SMC on a Mac, plug it in and restart the computer.

To switch off the MacBook, hold the power button down while pressing and holding Control, Option, and Shift for seven seconds. Hold the power button, the three keys, and the combination for an additional seven seconds. After a little delay, turn the power back on. The SMC for desktop Intel Macs will reset by turning off the machine. After disconnecting your MacBook Air, wait 15 seconds before plugging it back in and turning it on. Any issues with the Mac's Hot Corners function should be resolved when the SMC is reset.

Chapter 10

How to use Notes on Mac

Set up your Internet Accounts

You can use applications like Mail, Calendar, Contacts, and Notes after you have created Internet Accounts on your Mac. With this, you can use Notes with iCloud, Gmail, Outlook, and any other accounts you have.

1. To link your accounts with Notes, go to the **System Preferences > Internet Accounts menu option**. After that, check the box next to Notes for every account that you want to use.

2. As soon as you complete these steps, the sidebar on the left of the Notes app will update to include a folder for each account you have marked. You can see these folders by selecting **View > Show Folders** from the menu bar or by clicking the **Show Folders button** that is located in the toolbar.

Customize the Notes Toolbar

Notes, much like your other Mac applications, have a toolbar at the top that can be customized. This provides you with easy access various functions, including the ability to make a new note, add a table or checklist, enter media, and alter your view.

The steps:

1. Right-clicking in the toolbar area or selecting **View** from the menu bar and then selecting **Customize Toolbar** will allow you to adjust the buttons in the toolbar to correspond to the activities you will use most often.
2. The next step is to place the buttons in the toolbar where you want them by dragging them from the choices at the bottom. You are also free to rearrange those buttons in any way you see fit. When you are done, click the **Done** button.

Pick your view

Both **list** view and **gallery** view are available within the Notes application. To choose the view that will be used, go to the menu bar and click the **View**

button. In addition to that, the toolbar's **List** and **Gallery** buttons are at your disposal.

- The **List view** displays each of your notes as a list, complete with the note's title, the date it was created, and a snippet of its contents.
- When you switch to **Gallery view**, your notes will be presented in a grid structure with the same information but in a more expansive, thumbnail format.

Organize Notes with Folders

With the use of folders, the Notes app on your Mac allows you to arrange your information in a manner that is identical to how you organize files on your computer.

Create a folder

You can create folders within any of your accounts, in addition to the Internet Account folders that are shown on the sidebar. For instance, if you already have a business account, you are free to set up folders for your various projects.

To create a folder, do one of the following:

1. After choosing the account (folder), go to the bottom of the sidebar and select the **New Folder button**.

2. Select the folder, and then go to the menu bar and choose **File > New Folder**.

3. To create a new folder, go to the folder's account by clicking the three dots to the right of the folder's name.

4. Simply give your folder a name, then click the **Return key** on your keyboard.

Rename a Folder

- To rename a folder, click the three dots to its right, and then click **Rename Folder**. After giving the folder its new name, press the **Return key** on your keyboard.

Rearrange Folders

- To relocate a folder to a new place in the sidebar, pick the folder you want to move, and then drag & drop it into the new area.

Delete a Folder

- Click the three dots to the right of the folder you wish to remove, and then click the **Delete Folder button**.
- Finally, click the **OK** button to indicate that you want to delete the folder along with its contents. Alternatively, choose the folder, then go to the menu bar, pick Edit, and then click **Delete**.

Work with Notes

Here is how to deal with your notes, including how to create new notes and delete old ones that are no longer needed.

Create a note

- To make a new note, choose **File > New Note** from the menu bar or select the **Create a Note** button in the toolbar. Your new note will be added to the sidebar folder that is currently chosen when you create it. This is the default behavior. However, you can shift notes around as necessary.

Move a note

There are two straightforward approaches to moving a note:

- Right-click the mouse, move the pointer to the **Move to a menu** item, and then choose the desired place.
- To move the note from the list to the desired folder in the sidebar, just drag and drop the note.

Pin a note

You can "**pin**" a note to the board if you want it to remain at the very top of the list.

- Use the context menu to choose **Pin Note**.
- Make sure the note is selected, then go to the menu bar and choose **File > Pin Note**.

If you wish to unpin a note, use one of the techniques described above and choose the **Unpin Note option**.

Lock a note

You have the option of locking a note if you desire to safeguard its contents with a password.

The steps:

- Use the context menu to choose **Lock Note**.
- To lock the note, choose the note you wish to lock, and then click the **Lock button** in the toolbar.
- Make sure the note is selected, then go to the menu bar and choose **File > Lock Note**.
- After that, you should type in the password you want to use and click the OK button.
- The message will continue to be accessible until you lock it. To lock the note, click the **Lock button** on the toolbar when it is unlocked and then choose **Close All Locked Notes** from the drop-down menu.
- After you have locked it, you will be prompted to enter the password whenever you try to reopen it on any of your devices, including your Mac. You also have the option to unlock passwords on your Mac by using your Apple Watch.

- At this time, there is no method to recover a note password that has been forgotten. Use a password that is easy to recall or write it down and store it in a secure location.
- In addition, if you lock one note, the same password will be used for all subsequent notes you lock, regardless of whether you change it. You must keep this in mind, even though doing so will free you from having to remember a password for every note you want to secure.
- You can unlock a note by either clicking the **Remove Lock button** in the toolbar or by right-clicking the note and selecting the **Remove Lock** option from the context menu.

Delete a note

It is possible to erase a note in a few different ways. Just be sure that you want to eliminate it entirely since you won't get a notification asking you to confirm your decision.

The steps:

- Right-click, then choose the **Delete option.**
- Click the **Delete (trash can) button** located in the toolbar once the note has been selected.

- To delete the note, select it first, then go to **Edit > Delete** in the menu bar.

Format your notes

Text formatting options are available in Notes and comparable to those found in an outline. These options include a title, header, subheading, and body. After selecting the text you want to format, choose **Format** from the toolbar's menu or the Format button in the toolbar itself. In addition, you can use a numbered, dashed, or bulleted list format.

The steps:

1. Click the **Format button** in the top menu bar to apply formatting to your text.
2. Put your mouse over the **Font** option at the bottom to change things like **bold** or **italics**; the **Text** option to change the alignment or writing direction, and the Indentation option to change the amount of space between lines.

Sort your notes

Once you begin using Apple Notes, it is easy to quickly accumulate a large number of notes in each of your folders. If you know how to organize those notes, it will be much easier for you to locate the ones you need when you need them.

The steps:

- First, choose the folder you want to sort, then go to the **View menu** and select **Sort Folder By**.
- To sort the folder by a particular name, click the three dots to the right of the folder's name.

You have the option of arranging the notes included inside a folder according to the Title, the Date Edited, or the Date Created. After selecting the Date option, you will be given a choice to sort the results from most recent to oldest or vice versa. If you choose Title, you will be given the option to sort the results from A to Z or Z to A.

Search Notes

Make use of the app's Search function if you need to locate a note or attachment in a hurry inside the Notes app. Simply type in a term, and the results will appear very instantly.

- You can search across all of your accounts or just the one you have now chosen when you click the **magnifying glass icon** in the Search box. Thanks to this, you now have an excellent means of narrowing down your search right from the beginning.
- After entering the search word, your results will be shown in the notes list; these results will contain notes as well as any attachments that match the search.

Add items to your notes

You can connect a wide variety of objects to your notes, which is helpful whether you are making a list, organizing a project, or preparing for a vacation.

Add media to notes

Your notes include scanned papers, images, and drawings that you have taken with your iPhone, as well as photos that you have taken with your Mac. This is an excellent method for storing all of those different references to your notes together in one place.

The steps:

- Use the note's context menu to choose an action, then right-click anywhere inside the note body.
- Make sure the note is selected, then go to the toolbar and pick the **Media button.**

Add attachments to note

- Simply dragging an item from where it is now located into your note is the quickest and simplest method to add an attachment.
- You also have the option of using the "**reverse action**" to add these things to your notes. If you have a file open in Pages, for instance, you send a copy of it to Notes.

Browse attachments in Notes

One convenient location provides access to all the images, files, and other items attached to your notes.

- Click the **Attachments button** on your toolbar.
- When you are there, choose one of the tabs at the top of the screen that corresponds to the kind of file you want to view, and then browse for the

file. You can also use the search bar that is located at the very top of the Notes page to locate entries that include a certain term.

Add tables to notes

You can also use tables in Notes, which is excellent news if you use tables to keep your stuff organized.

The steps:

1. To insert a table, choose **Format > Table** from the menu bar or click the **Table button** in the toolbar.
2. To modify the table by including or removing columns or rows, pick the table, and then click the three dots at the top of each column or on the left side of each row. That row or column will be highlighted as a result. After that, choose an alternative by clicking the arrow next to it.
3. To remove a table, select it and then press the **Delete button** on your keyboard.

Add checklists to notes

Using a checklist in Notes is a fantastic method to generate a list of things that need to be done or items that need to be purchased.

1. To add a checklist, choose **Format > Checklist** from the menu bar or click the **Checklist button** in the toolbar.
2. After you have entered one item into the list, just use the **Return key** on your keyboard to add another item.

Share your notes

You can share notes with other users or with other applications. This makes it simple for you to cooperate in whichever method best suits your needs.

Add people

It is easy to do this if you have a particular note that you want another person to be allowed to access or update on your behalf.

The steps:

1. Select the name of your note and click the **Add People button** in the toolbar or go to **File > Add People To** from the menu bar.
2. Choose the means through which you will communicate the letter to the recipient, such as sending it via Messages, Email, or AirDrop.

3. Select the option that you want next to Permission. Your options are: Only people you invite can make changes or only people you invite can see.

4. If the Add field is there, fill it out; after clicking the **Share button**, follow the on-screen instructions to add your friend to your note.

Use your Share Menu

1. To send a note using the Share Menu extensions with your Mac, choose **File > Share** from the menu bar or click the **Share button** located in the toolbar.

2. Follow the on-screen instructions to email or share your message once you have selected the appropriate app or service.

Chapter 11

How to use Spotlight on the Mac

You can search for almost anything on your Mac using Apple's Spotlight search tool, which makes the process very simple. A Spotlight search is different from a search conducted in the Finder in that, in addition to searching your computer for downloaded files and stored files, Spotlight also searches the internet for material like news, the weather, and anything related to your search.

What can Spotlight help you locate?

You should be able to locate just about anything on your Mac with the assistance of Spotlight. It indexes the contents of the hard disk on your Mac to make it simpler to discover information like documents, emails, applications, music, and contacts, among other types of data. Additionally, it can assist you in searching for information on the web, calculating equations, and, as of the release of High Sierra, it can even find the information you need for your flights.

Accessing and Using Spotlight

The steps:

1. In the top menu bar, you will see a button labeled "**Spotlight.**" This button resembles a magnifying glass. Alternatively, you can use the keyboard shortcut, that is **Command + Space**. The field for searching with Spotlight will appear in the screen's center.
2. Enter the search terms you want to use. While you write, Spotlight will display the relevant results.
3. If you're having trouble finding what you're searching for using Spotlight, you may customize its search results to suit your requirements better. You can also block Spotlight from scanning certain areas on your hard drive to avoid revealing information you'd like to remain confidential by excluding specific locations.

Customize Spotlight Results

The steps:

1. Select the **Apple menu button** in the screen's upper left-hand corner.

2. Navigate to the **System Preferences menu**.
3. Select **Spotlight** from the menu.
4. To modify the content that Spotlight will show, click the checkbox that is located next to the category. Those results will be shown if they have a checkbox next to them; if it does not, those results will not be presented.

Hide Content from Spotlight Search

You can tell Spotlight not to look in particular areas, which is helpful if you store sensitive documents in a given location but do not want them uncovered during a search.

The steps:

1. Make your selection by clicking the **Apple menu button** in your screen's upper left corner.
2. Navigate to the **System Preferences menu**.
3. Select **Spotlight** from the menu.
4. Navigate to the tab labeled "**Privacy.**"
5. Select the "**add**" **option** from the menu.
6. Select the object that you do not want Spotlight to look for by clicking on it.
7. Select **Choose**.

8. Then add more things to the list by repeating the steps.

How to Use "Hey Siri"

Perhaps what most user don't known is that many of Apple's new Macs also support hands-free "**Hey Siri,**" meaning users no longer need to click the menu bar icon or press a keyboard shortcut before they can begin speaking to the digital assistant. This feature is available on Apple's new Macs series, including the MacBook Air 2022.

How to Enable "Hey Siri" without Touching the Keyboard on a Mac

The steps:

1. Navigate to the **System Preferences menu** by clicking the **Apple** Menu located in the upper left-hand corner of the screen.
2. Select the **Siri** symbol from the drop-down menu located in the preferences window.
3. Check the option next to **Listen for "Hey Siri"** to activate the feature.

4. After clicking **Continue**, proceed with the setup procedure for Siri by voice repeating the instructions that are shown on the screen.

5. After loading the preference window, click the **Done** button.

Saying "Hey Siri" is all that is required to activate the digital assistant so that you can pose a question to it or issue an order once you have activated the capability.

Chapter 12

How to use Live Text on Mac

Live Text is a feature in the MacBook Air 2022 running macOS 12 Monterey. It can instantly recognize text whenever it appears in a picture inside Safari, Photos, Preview, Quick Look, and other applications. This makes it possible for you to simply copy and share the text.

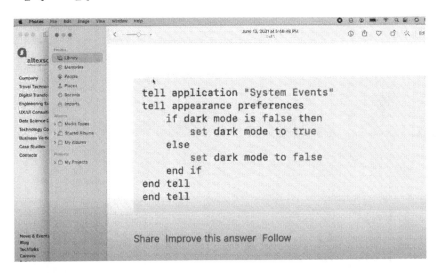

The steps:

1. Using Photos, Preview, or Quick Look, locate a picture that has text.
2. Using Safari, download an image from the internet that contains the text.

3. When you move the pointer over the part of the picture that contains the text, the cursor will transform into a tool that allows you to pick the text. By clicking and dragging the mouse over the text, you highlight it.

4. After that, pick an action for the highlighted text from the contextual menu that displays when you right-click the text. Look It Up, Translate, Search with Google, Copy, and Share need should all be options available to users.

5. If you copied the text, open another application on your device that allows you to enter text, then right-click the editing window and pick the **Paste option**.

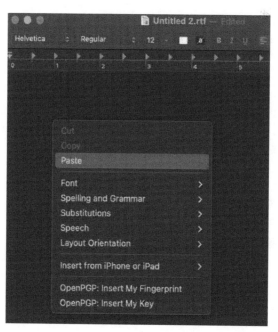

Interact with Text in a Photo Using Live Text in Preview

You can copy and use the text displayed on an image by using the **Live Text** feature in **Preview**. You could, for instance, copy the text from a sign by the side of the road and then paste it into an email or a text message. You can make a call, access a webpage, or send an email using the phone number, website, or email address shown in a photo.

The steps:

1. On your Mac, use the **Preview app** and choose a picture or image that has text to open it.
2. Move the cursor so that it is over the text you want to choose, and then drag it across.
3. Choose one of the following actions to take:
   - To copy text, right-click your selection, pick **Control-Copy**, and then hit **Enter** (or press **Command-C**). After that, you can copy the content and paste it into a different document or app.

- Determine the meaning of the text by looking it up: Control-click the item you want to look up, and then pick the text.

- To translate text, control-click the selection you want to translate, choose to **Translate [text]**, and then pick a language from the drop-down menu. Be aware that translation is not accessible in all languages, and it is possible that it is not available in certain countries or areas.

- **Conduct a search on the internet for the text:** Control-click the items you want to search for, and then pick the appropriate online search engine.

- **Discuss the reading content with other people:** Control-click the text you wish to share, choose the **Share menu item**, and then pick the method you want to use.

- **Call a phone number:** Control-click your selection or click the down arrow ∨, and then pick whether you want to phone the number, create a **FaceTime video or audio call**, or send a message to the number. You can accomplish any of these by clicking the appropriate button.

- **Send an email to the following address:** Control-click the item you want to choose or click the down arrow ∨, and then pick whether you want to initiate a FaceTime video or audio call, write an email, or add the email address to your Contacts list.

Chapter 13

How to Create a New Shortcut

The gallery will be the first location you visit when opening Shortcuts for the first time. This gives you access to a comprehensive library of pre-made shortcuts that you may choose from. These are arranged in a way that will make it easier for you to discover what you need.

There is a category that can assist you with anything you need, whether it be something to help you organize your images, generate GIFs, or receive some assistance with focusing and increasing your productivity. When you open your sidebar, you will see several extra choices, including All Shortcuts, Quick Actions, and the Menu Bar.

All of the shortcuts you have built will be synchronized across your Mac and your iOS device when you use Shortcuts. On the other hand, the Mac is the only platform that supports two more actions.

Creating a shortcut may be as simple as dragging certain activities on a window, like branches on a tree. Nevertheless, you can create shortcuts for resizing images, opening two programs in split-screen mode, and much more.

The steps:

1. Launch **Shortcuts**. You can locate this in the "**Applications**" **folder** on your computer. You can also look for it using the Spotlight search tool on your computer. Access this by hitting Command and Space Bar on your keyboard, or you can click the magnifying glass symbol on your keyboard if it's there.

2. After starting the program, choose the **plus sign +** located in the upper right-hand corner of the screen.

3. Using this information, you will be able to create your shortcut. You can use the search tool to zero in on the specific activity you wish to carry out; you can also use it to piece together the options you want to personalize your shortcut.

4. At this point, you have the option of naming your shortcut and personalizing it by assigning it a certain color and selecting icons to make it easily identifiable. Click anywhere outside of the window when you are ready to close it. When you exit this window and return to the list of shortcuts, you will see that your newly created shortcut has been added.

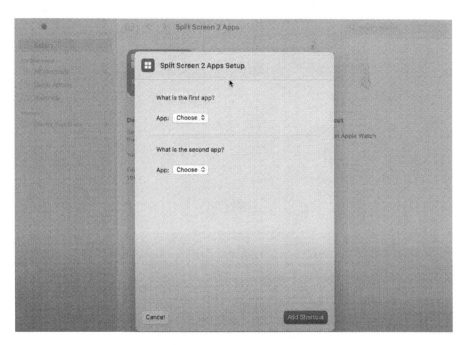

Adding a Shortcut to the Menu Bar

After you have made your shortcut, you may want to consider pinning it to your menu bar so that you can quickly and easily access it in the future. This is particularly the case if it is a function or procedure that is used regularly.

Set up a Shortcut as a Quick Action

The following actions must be taken to use a shortcut as a Quick Action; these processes are virtually similar to those required for adding a shortcut to the menu bar. When using your Mac, using shortcuts is a straight-forward and efficient approach to cut down on wasted time. When you get more experience with the tool, you will be able to personalize it more, allowing you to design more intricate and advanced workflow.

Create a Custom Shortcut

Using the Shortcuts software on a Mac, it is simple to create a new shortcut that is specific to your needs:

1. The first thing you should do is add a new shortcut to your collection of shortcuts.
2. Then add actions in the shortcut editor.
3. Test your newly created shortcut by running it.

Gallery

Since the Gallery is a good starting point for becoming acquainted with Shortcuts, it is the first part that can be found in the app. It is a compilation of shortcuts arranged into categories according to the many functions they perform.

These categories consist of:

- **Starter Shortcuts** are fundamental yet may come in useful, such as sending a message to someone with your most current picture.
- **Accessibility Shortcuts**: These shortcuts are mostly geared toward health and emergencies; for example, you can quickly send a message and your location to people on your emergency contact list or keep track of the prescription you take.
- **Works well with Siri**: Shortcuts that can be accessed hands-free with Siri might be helpful. This collection has a shortcut that, in addition

to playing a podcast for you, will also ask Siri to provide you with the current weather and the amount of time it will take you to go to work.

- **Wonderful Widget Shortcuts**: These shortcuts can be accessed quickly and easily via the Shortcuts app widget. For example, there is a shortcut that allows you to **"play the full current album."**
- **Share Sheet Shortcuts**: These shortcuts allow you to save, share, or update the material you are currently reading in a streamlined manner. You can modify a Safari website, convert a webpage to a PDF file, or add a book to your wish list using some shortcuts.
- **Keyboard shortcuts for Apple Music**: For accessing all aspects of Apple Music. Open up genre playlists, play an artist's music, discuss what you have been listening to this week, and so much more.
- Shortcut links for sharing content on Twitter and Instagram, accessible from inside the Mail. The use of specific shortcuts, such as the **"AirDrop screenshot"** shortcut, will make it

somewhat less challenging to transmit content to other people.

The Gallery also has other collections, most of which are centered on productivity. There are over a dozen more, but some examples include **Get Stuff Done** and **Get Organized** in addition to **Work from Anywhere**. After you have become familiar with the Gallery and its many shortcuts, you will be able to begin creating yours.

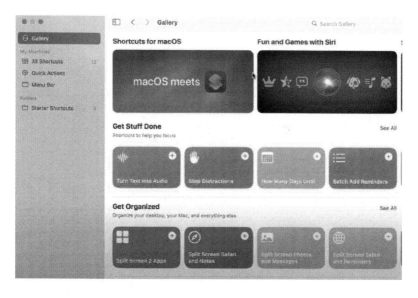

Delete Shortcuts

When it is time to move on from a shortcut, it is simple to erase it from your computer. You can do one of the following with the Shortcuts app:

1. First, pick the shortcut you want to delete, go to **Edit > Delete**, and click the **Delete Shortcut button**.
2. To delete a shortcut, first select it, then press **Command and Delete**, and last click the **Delete Shortcut button**.

Chapter 14

How to use Finder on a MacBook Air

The native Mac graphical user interface and file manager is called **Finder**. At the top of the screen is the primary Finder menu bar, which is static. It has several settings that enable users to access all the functions on a Mac. In addition, Finder serves as a file manager (like Windows Explorer in Windows Operating System). Typically, the **directory of files** and **shortcuts** is located on the left panel, while the **stored content** and files are shown on the right side. As a result, it enables us to view every piece of stored data and directory that the Mac already has. In addition, you can create new files and folders using the MacBook Finder. Through the Mac Finder search, you may also get to a certain place. For a better browsing experience, you can even preview your files and documents on the side panel.

Where is Finder?

Now that you are aware of how crucial the Mac Finder is let's find out where it is on the Mac and how to get to it. Since Finder is one of the most crucial elements on a Mac, its shortcut is automatically included in the dock. However, the Finder main menu, located in the top panel of the screen, is another way to access it.

The steps:

1. For convenience, the dock by default includes a Finder icon. To access its functions, double-click it.
2. You may also access the top-of-the-screen main menu after choosing the **Mac Finder icon**. To open a new tab and explore your Mac's storage, navigate to **File > New Tab**.

New Finder Window
New Folder
New Folder with Selection
New Smart Folder
New Burn Folder
New Tab
Open
Open With
Print

3. This will cause the screen to display a new window. You can navigate to whatever you like or use the shortcuts on the left panel to get there.

Common Features and Mac Finder Solutions

The Mac Finder benefits users in a variety of ways.

They include the following:

1. Mac Shortcuts and Finder Icon

The happy Mac symbol represents the Mac finder shortcut, which is available on the dock. It is just one click to launch the Mac's File Finder. In addition, the MacBook Finder offers a ton of keyboard shortcuts for quick access to its most used functions.

- **Command + N**: Launches a new window
- **Command + T**: Launches a new tab
- **Command + F**: Launches the Finder's search window.

- **Command + I:** Brings up the Finder's info window.
- **Command + Option + S:** This toggles the sidebar on or off.
- To get the icon/list/column/cover flow view, use Command + 1/2/3/4.
- The iCloud Drive is opened by pressing **Command + Shift + I.**
- **Command + Shift + D:** Launches the desktop application
- Pressing **Command + Shift + O** will launch the **Documents folder.**
- Pressing **Command + Shift + F** will bring up the "**All My Files**" folder.
- The Downloads folder is opened by pressing **Command + Shift + L.**

2. **Use the Preview Pane**

Use the Finder Mac's preview window to save time and improve your experience. If the functionality is not enabled, choose "**Show Preview**" from the **View** menu under the Finder's main menu. After that, you will see a preview of your images, movies, documents, and other files on the side panel when you open the Finder.

3. Change the way your files are shown

The way files are seen on the Finder can also be modified. Observe the many display options on the Finder's toolbar, including an icon, list, column, and cover flow. You can choose an option of your own or even use one of the shortcuts mentioned above. To switch the perspective, press Command together with one of the 1/2/3/4 numeric keys.

To further personalize the Finder's appearance select **View > Show View Options** from the main menu. Here you can modify the Finder's icon size, grid spacing, and other display settings.

4. Use the Sidebar on Finder

One of File Finder most helpful features is the sidebar. The sidebar should ideally include favorite places, tags, shortcuts, etc. For a better user experience, you can also personalize the sidebar of the Finder Window on Mac. For access, choose **Finder > Preferences > Sidebar**. To add a folder's easy access, just drag it and drop it in the sidebar.

5. To locate files, use the Search Box

Even without knowing their precise position, you can easily locate certain files and folders using the search box. The Mac Finder already has a search bar at the top-right corner. You can also start the Mac Finder search by using the **Command + F keys**. Simply click on it > input the name of the file or folder you are looking for, and it will display the appropriate results.

6. Delete files using Finder

With the aid of the Mac Finder, you can also delete any file or folder if you wish to. To do this, start the Finder on your MacBook and search for the files you want to remove. Alternatively, you can utilize the search bar to achieve the same result. Right-click the files or folders you want to choose. Select "**Move to Trash**" from the context menu to remove the chosen content.

Tips for Making the Most of the Mac Finder

In addition to the aforementioned elements and functionalities, Finder can be used in various ways.

Here's how:

1. Opening Finder on a Mac

To access Finder, use the keyboard shortcuts **Command + F**. Don't panic and carry out the following actions if you can't locate the Mac Finder icon on the dock:

- Select **Go > Go to Folder** from the main menu and type "**/System/Library/CoreServices/**".
- Find the Mac Finder icon in the list of Core Services and drag it to the dock.

How to Shut Down and Restart Finder on a Mac

You can quickly resolve any problems with the Mac Finder window by relaunching it.

1. To restart Finder on your Mac, go to the main menu and choose **Apple > Force Quit Finder**.
2. Accept the pop-up window's request to compel the Finder window to close.
3. After the Mac Finder window has been closed, you can right-click on its icon in the dock. You

may restart Finder by selecting it from the context menu.

Determining a Search Type

Both **Spotlight** and **Finder** provide advanced search features that allow you to limit the results based on various criteria.

1. To see results, key in a search term into the Finder's search field.
2. By doing this, the appropriate **"tag"** that serves as the main filter will be added.
3. Directly next to it, you can specify the search type and extension. The **+ and - buttons** is used to add or remove filters.

How to Change a Finder's Default Folder

Choose a particular folder as the default option in the Finder if it is one that you visit often. In this method, the default folder will always be opened when you run the Finder app.

1. To achieve this, visit the Finder Preferences tab by selecting the **main menu > Finder > Preferences**.

2. Select the "New Finder windows display" opt-ion from the dropdown menu on the General tab. You can then proceed to select the default folder.

How to Rename Multiple Files and Undo it

The ability to rename several files at once is one of the finest features of the Mac's file Finder. You may save time and creating a group of files and arranging them in this manner. However, you may quickly reverse the name if you wish.

1. Open **Mac Finder** and choose the files you want to rename, choose **"rename files"** by clicking the gear symbol in the toolbar.
2. To distinguish between these files, choose to replace, format, or add text. You can add the name and index to each file if you select the format.
3. Click the **"Rename" button** after making the necessary choices and adding a text or index to files.
4. To reverse the rename in case of a mistake, hit the **Command + Z buttons** simultaneously. You can also choose **"Undo"** or **"Undo Ren-**

ame" from the Edit menu under the main menu.

How to Show or Hide the All My Files Icon

You've probably come across the "**All My Files**" **option** when using the Finder window on a Mac. All the files saved on a Mac are often shown in the Finder's default window. The option is also mentioned in the sidebar of Finder, which you may display or conceal whenever you want.

The steps:

1. First, choose **Preferences** from the Finder menu at the top.
2. Open the **Finder Preferences window** and choose the "**Sidebar**" **option**.
3. Several options are available under the heading "**Show these things in the sidebar.**" The "**All My Files**" **option** can be enabled or disabled to display or conceal its icon in the Finder sidebar.

Troubleshooting Common Finder Issues

Although using a Mac finder is simple, there is a potential that you may run into some unfavorable problems.

Here are they:

1. The Mac Finder Does Not Work

One of the most useful tools in the Mac finder is the search tab, which enables us to hunt for any file or folder on the computer.

Here are some of the solutions:

- **Restart Mac**

The quickest solution for Mac Finder search troubles is to shut off Finder right now or select to force it to close. Later, you can right-click the Mac Finder icon on the dock menu and choose to restart it.

- **Verify the search query**

As you are aware, the Finder search on a Mac can be used in a variety of ways. You can search for a file using the advanced search options by using particular keywords, extensions, or other criteria. If the search option doesn't appear to function, you can remove a sub-query by clicking the "-" **minus symbol**. Additionally, confirm that you started with the correct query.

- **Change Finder Preferences**

Consider going to the Mac finder's Preferences if nothing else seems to work to improve the search function. Select the **"When searching" dropdown menu** from the Advanced settings in Finder Preferences. It should ideally be the folder you are now viewing. To repair the Mac finder search, modify these settings to your chosen option.

- **Finder on Mac not responding**

The Mac Finder freezes up much too often for various reasons. Follow these recommendations for a better Finder Mac experience.

- **Use terminal**

The Mac has a specific core component called **Terminal** that enables users to provide the system instructions. Therefore, use the **Terminal** for help if you wish to terminate finder on a Mac. Search for

Terminal using Spotlight. To terminate Finder on a Mac, open the program and use the command **"killall -KILL Finder."**

- Restart your Mac

You can try restarting the Mac if the issue persists. To do this, choose **Restart** from the Apple menu, and confirm your decision. You can also accomplish that by simultaneously pressing the **Command, Shift, and Power keys**.

- Mac Finder Slow

The Mac finder might slow down if your MacBook is overloaded or if you are using an old version of macOS. Here's a quick workaround for the sluggish Mac Finder problem.

- Examine Mac Storage

Finder can become sluggish or unresponsive if your Mac system is short on free space. Go to the desktop, click the **Apple** Menu, choose **This Mac > About**, and then select the **"Storage" option**. You can check how much space your Mac has here. If there isn't enough free space, you can delete some files to increase the amount of Mac storage that is accessible.

Chapter 15

How to Set Up FaceTime on a Mac

It's simple to make a video or voice call using FaceTime. A built-in or linked microphone and camera are all that is required, along with a broadband internet connection.

Setting up FaceTime on a Mac

You don't need to download anything else since the FaceTime program is already installed on your Mac, and the setup is really simple:

1. Click the **FaceTime icon** on the menu bar to launch the FaceTime application, or **press** ⌘ + **Space and enter FaceTime.**

2. To activate FaceTime, click **Turn On** if it isn't already.

3. Enter your Apple ID and password to log in.

4. Navigate to **FaceTime > Preferences** to choose how you can be accessed on FaceTime. You can choose here whether you wish to use FaceTime with all of the email addresses associated with your Apple account (for example, you might not want people who have your work email address to contact you via FaceTime).

5. Uncheck any email addresses you don't want to be associated with on FaceTime calls.

6. Simply visit **System Preferences > Apple ID > Name, Phone, Email > Reachable** and click the + symbol to add an email address to the list. The modifications will immediately show up in the FaceTime settings.

What you need for a Mac FaceTime video chat

The majority of Macs are built to support FaceTime calls, so all you need to do is make sure all the necessary accessories are connected:

- A good internet connection with a minimum download and upload speed of 128 kbps.
- An integrated or wireless camera (MacBooks and iMacs come with one, but you need to purchase it separately for the Mac Mini and Mac Pro).
- A microphone (most Macs have them, but you can also plug in a headset with a mic for better quality).
- Apple ID for logging into FaceTime.

How to call someone on FaceTime

FaceTime for Mac is simple to use as long as both you and the person you're calling have a good internet connection, are signed in, and have the app open:

1. Open the **Contacts app**.
2. Look up the individual you want to call. A name, phone number, or email address may be used to search.
3. Select the option to initiate a FaceTime call by clicking on the contact's profile (it looks like a video camera icon).

4. Making a FaceTime call is now easier on macOS Monterey due to shared links. To invite individuals, click **New FaceTime** once you've opened FaceTime and enter their phone numbers or email addresses. Alternatively, you can generate a link by clicking on the **Create a Link** option and send it to anybody.

How to accept calls on your Mac using FaceTime

The steps:

1. First, a pop-up window will appear. You'll see a notification in the upper-right area if FaceTime has been closed.
2. If you have the caller's information in the Contacts app, the notice will let you know who is calling.
3. Click **Accept** if you want to communicate with them.
4. If you get a FaceTime link on macOS Monterey, you can join by clicking on the link.
5. Click the **red handset symbol** to hang up the call.

What does group FaceTime entail?

Group FaceTime is for connecting to several people, such as a family reunion or business conference. Up to 32 users can participate in a single active video conversation on the FaceTime app.

To place a group FaceTime call:

1. Launch the **FaceTime app** and choose "**New FaceTime.**"
2. Type the contact information—name, phone number, or email address—of each person you want to FaceTime in a group, separated by commas. Alternatively, choose each one of your contacts separately.
3. To start the group FaceTime video conference, click the **green video icon**.
4. To invite extra people to a Group FaceTime session already in progress, click in the lower-left corner of the window to reveal the sidebar, click **Add Person** to enter their details, and then pick **Add**.
5. When someone joins a group FaceTime chat on macOS Monterey, their videos will appear as identically sized tiles in a grid layout. One's tile

is highlighted to indicate they are speaking. The Portrait mode in macOS 12 Monterey (click your **tile > Video Effects**) might also be useful.

How to Stop Unwanted FaceTime Calls?

FaceTime also lets you quickly ban any caller at any time:

The steps:

1. Start **FaceTime**.
2. Use your Apple ID to log in.
3. Look up the name of the caller you want to ban.
4. Right-click on a number and select **Block This Caller**.

Use FaceTime Links

FaceTime links, introduced in macOS 12 Monterey, allow you to transmit a link to every participant before the conversation starts, making it simpler to prepare for FaceTime calls. You may invite friends who use Android and Windows phones to the call using FaceTime Links. Users with the most recent version of **Chrome** or **Edge**, can also join the conversation through their browser.

The steps:

1. On a Mac running macOS Monterey, launch the **FaceTime application**.
2. To access the sharing menu, click **Create Link** $\mathcal{O}$. The link can then be copied or you can choose a different sharing method.
3. After generating the connection link, it appears on the FaceTime window's sidebar.
4. Double-click the FaceTime Link in the sidebar or click the FaceTime icon ◼️ next to it to initiate the call. After that, you click the **Join** button.
5. Other people need to be allowed to join the call when they access the FaceTime link and click **Join**.
   - Select the checkbox next ✅ to their name to allow them to join the call.
   - Click the **Decline** button ✖️ next to their name to reject their invitation to join the call.

- After they've joined, click the delete button ⊗ within 30 seconds to cut them off from the call.

6. Click the **Info** button ⓘ in the sidebar next to the link, and then click **Delete Link**, to remove a FaceTime link. When a link is deleted, you are no longer informed whenever someone clicks on it, and whoever uses the deleted link will only see that they are awaiting authorization.

7. A FaceTime connection can also be established in the Calendar app. When creating a new event, choose FaceTime by clicking the Face-Time icon next to "**Add Location or Video Call.**" Everyone you invite will be aware of the precise location and time of the meeting, thanks to the smooth FaceTime connection integration with the Calendar event.

Join a Call Using a FaceTime Link

The steps:

1. Select the **FaceTime option**. The link opens in your web browser if you're using a device that is not compatible with the FaceTime app. The most

recent versions of Microsoft Edge and Google Chrome enable FaceTime connections on Android and Windows devices.

2. To join the call through a web browser, you must first enter your name and then click **Continue** afterward.

3. Select **Join**, and then wait to be allowed in.

Screen Sharing on FaceTime

For so long, FaceTime on macOS lacked a screen sharing capability, but Apple finally included it in macOS 12 Monterey, which comes with the 2022 MacBook Air. You can begin screen sharing with FaceTime if all participants run a compatible Operating system.

Share Your Screen on FaceTime Using SharePlay

Each participant's device must run macOS 12 Monterey, iOS 15.1, iPadOS 15.1, or a later version to share a screen. It's important to ensure everyone on the call has the appropriate software installed since, at this time, you cannot share your screen with

Windows or Android users. Screen sharing features are not available if even one participant does not have a suitable device.

Here's how to screen share on macOS 12 Monterey using FaceTime:

1. Start **FaceTime**.
2. Select a recent contact or click **New FaceTime** to start a new call.
3. Click the **SharePlay button** when the call has connected.
4. Select **Screen** to share your complete screen or **Window** to share a single window. If you select **Window**, you will then be prompted to pick which app to share from.
5. Up until you decide to end the conversation, other callers will be able to see the screen or window you shared. From the same **SharePlay option**, you can stop screen sharing or change what other people view.

Use Share Play to Watch and Listen Together on FaceTime

You can integrate TV programs, movies, and music into FaceTime sessions with SharePlay in macOS 12 Monterey. Thanks to simultaneous playback and shared controls, you can also have a real-time connection with everyone in the conversation. The audio is automatically adjusted with smart loudness so you can keep conversing while viewing or listening.

Be aware that certain SharePlay-compatible applications need a subscription to use them. Not every country or location has access to every feature and piece of information.

Watch Video Together

While in a FaceTime conversation with someone else, you can view movies and television programs. The same moments may be seen at the same time, and everyone on the call can use the shared playback controls to push Play or Pause if they all have access to the video content (via a subscription or free trial, for example). The volume of the program or movie is automatically adjusted so you can converse while watching.

The steps:

1. Open the **Apple TV app** ⬛ on your Mac and begin viewing a movie or program while on a FaceTime chat.
2. Verify that you want to use SharePlay. After that, SharePlay launches on its own.
3. The content can be seen simultaneously by everyone on the call who has access to it. Participants who lack access are encouraged to do so (through a subscription, a transaction, or a free trial, if available).

Everyone can use the playback controls on their Apple devices to play, stop, rewind, or fast-forward in real-time while viewing together.

Listen to Music Together

FaceTime calls allow you to come together and enjoy music with other people. Suppose everyone participating in the call has the necessary access to the music. In that case, they can all simultaneously hear the song, see its title and what comes next, and use the shared controls to stop playback, rearrange tracks, add songs to the queue, and go on to the next track. You can also converse while listening since the music level is automatically adjusted to allow for this.

The steps:

1. To play music in the **Music app** 🎵 while in a FaceTime chat on your Mac, drag the cursor over any song or album, then click the **Play button** ▶. Confirm that you want to use SharePlay if this is your first time using it. After that, SharePlay launches on its own. The next time you want to use SharePlay for Music, you will be asked to choose **Start Only for Me**.
The music begins playing simultaneously for everyone on the call who can hear it and has access to it. People who lack access are encouraged to do so (through a subscription, a transaction, or a free trial, if available).

2. While everyone is listening, anybody on the call may manage the shared Playing Next queue, check lyrics, and control playback (pause the music, go to the next song, and more).

What is Shared with You?

With macOS 12 Monterey, the **Shared with You function** was made available. It syncs information shared with you, such as links and photographs, to the appropriate applications. The following applications specifically support Shared with You:

- Messages
- Safari
- Photos
- Music
- TV
- News
- Podcasts

You can use this feature to go back and forth across your discussions to access shared information by going straight to the **Shared with You** function. Additionally, it enables you to respond immediately and carry on a dialogue with the individual who provided you with the item.

Turn off "Shared with You" in Each App

You can either deactivate the functionality entirely or only on specific applications.

To turn off the functionality of a particular app:

1. Launch the supported app, e.g. Messages.
2. In the menu bar, click **Messages, and then choose Preferences**.
3. Select the tab **Shared with You**. Uncheck the boxes next to the applications whose material you do not wish to share.

You can also completely turn off the functionality for that application by navigating to:

1. Click the **Shared with You tab** under Preferences in your preferred app.
2. Press the **Off button**.

How to Stop Receiving FaceTime Calls

You can either turn off FaceTime or log out of the program if you no longer want to receive FaceTime calls on your Mac:

The steps:

1. Start **FaceTime**.
2. In the menu bar, choose **FaceTime > Preferences > Sign out or FaceTime Off**.

3. Turn FaceTime ON or log back in to make or receive calls again.

In some situations, you just want to reduce interruptions while working or doing other crucial duties on your Mac. Try **Focus** on this situation. The app allows you to temporarily silence all noise for however long or how little time you choose. Additionally, it enables you to design your productivity calendar with pre-set **"work & rest"** periods so that you can quickly resume your job after a break.

With **Focus**, you can carefully control what you block: e.g., whole websites and applications or just a single page on a given website. When you attempt to access a website or program that has been restricted, a gray screen with words of encouragement to stay productive will appear (you can choose from an extensive catalog of quotes or create your own).

What Should be done when FaceTime isn't Working?

If you encounter a FaceTime problem, there are a few things to check. Make sure your Apple ID is active first and that both the caller and you have the correct contact information (emails or phone numbers must be associated with your Apple ID for a FaceTime call to go through).

If it still doesn't work, make sure your email address is confirmed in FaceTime's preferences (if it isn't, look for the email verification option and follow the steps). Additionally, ensure that all the checkboxes next to the phone numbers and email addresses in Preferences are ticked.

Your time zone might sometimes be the source of the issue. Make sure the country you select in Face-Time Preferences is the right one. The area where your FaceTime account is registered should correspond with the location on your Mac. Check your time zone in System Preferences. Go to **System Preferences > Date & Time > Set Automatically > click on Time Zone > choose the closest city to resolve this**.

Finally, make sure you're connected to the internet and the speed is good enough (at least 128 kbps, or 1 Mbps for HD FaceTime video calls).

Fixing SharePlay not working in FaceTime

On macOS 12 Monterey and later, FaceTime is unquestionably the best option for SharePlay. Users now have access to the SharePlay feature, which allows them to view movies, listen to music, and share their screen during FaceTime group chat. Here are a few things to look into if SharePlay is not functioning as expected:

- Verify that SharePlay is turned on by going to **FaceTime Preferences > SharePlay**.
- Confirm that SharePlay is supported by the app you want to use for a SharePlay session. Only a few applications, like Apple TV and Apple Music, now support SharePlay.
- Verify that each participant has a subscription. All parties must have an active Apple TV subscription to view a movie via FaceTime.

Chapter 16

How to Split Screen

Split View enables you to run two programs simultaneously on your Mac without manually moving and resizing windows. A single window isn't always enough, particularly when working from home. Having many windows open makes it easier to transition between jobs.

Sometimes you need a lot of things around, whether it's to watch movies while working, go through data to generate a report, or have a chat window open while exploring. The process of navigating between full-screen programs may be tedious and time-consuming.

The steps:

1. Launch the two applications you want to use in split-screen mode. Check to be sure none of the windows you want to utilize is in full-screen.
2. Place your mouse on the top-left green button of one of the desired windows. Hold your mo-

use pointer over the window until a drop-down option appears.

3. Select either the tile window on the screen's left or on its right. On your Mac, the split-screen mode will start up immediately.

4. Other active windows will appear on the other side of the screen. Select the second window for the split view.

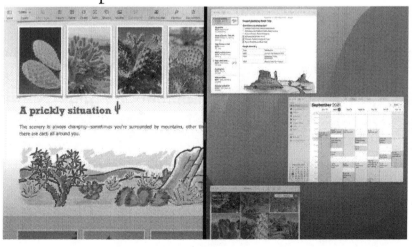

5. To change the size of the windows, use the slider in the screen's center. Split View enables simultaneous viewing of both windows.

Adjusting Split View

- You can change how much each app's screen occupies by using the Split View. You don't have to split it equally, which comes in handy when looking at a web page with a quirky design or having an additional room when working on a big spreadsheet. Also, be careful that certain applications have minimum width requirements that prevent you from resizing the bar.
- Click and hold an app's Title Bar and drag it to the other side to change the position of the windows.
- The resolution of the entire window can be adjusted if you feel they are too small.

Accessing Mission Control in a Split-Screen View

With split-screen mode, switching between the two windows is now simple. Use **Mission Control** to access your desktop if necessary. Use the **F3 key or**

Control + Up Arrow to activate **Mission Control**. Additionally, you can program motions for your Magic Mouse and Magic Trackpad.

- Wizard Trackpad using three or four fingers to swipe up
- Magic Mouse: Tap twice with both fingers.

Make sure the settings are configured properly. To achieve this, pick the aforementioned motions in **Apple Menu > System Preferences Mouse/ Trackpad.**

Why is my MacBook Air Unable to Use the Split Screen?

The steps:

1. First, make sure full screen mode is not turned on. The split screen is only supported by the default window view. Check if displays have separate spaces enabled in **System Preferences > Mission Control** to determine if that is the issue. If not, do so right now.
2. If you can't see that option in the **Mission Control** menu, ensure your operating system is

upgraded to macOS 12 Monterey or later. You can find out what OS version is presently installed on your machine by choosing **About this Mac** from the Apple icon in the upper left menu. Update if you are using an older macOS version on the Software Update screen.

3. Take note that not all programs support split displays. If you have done everything else and it still doesn't work, it is probable that the app doesn't support split-screen mode and won't tile in that mode.

How to use other apps in Split View

On a Mac, **Mission Control** can be used to open other applications.

The steps:

1. Open **Mission Control**.
2. To move between Split View and other windows, click the thumbnail at the top.

How Can I Leave Split Screen Mode?

The Split Screen functionality can be easily disabled. Here are the steps to follow:

1. To display the window choices, just move the mouse pointer to the top of the screen.
2. At this point, you must choose the full-screen option in one of the windows.
3. Afterwards, the particular window will close the Split view and the other window will instantly transition into the full-screen view.

Picture-in-Picture Mode: How to Use

Picture-in-Picture works well for multitasking, particularly if you want to view a movie while performing a different task on your Mac.

Multitask Effortlessly with Picture-in-Picture Mode

Here are some of the things that will make this function work well:

- Working while concurrently watching YouTube. You can sometimes find whole movies on YouTube, or perhaps you need to view a YouTube video to finish work on a Mac. Picture-in-Picture mode enables you to view the movie and continue working on other tasks at the same time.

- **Using a floating window to watch movies and videos.** There is no better way to view a movie while carrying out other tasks. To have the movie hover in the bottom right corner of your screen while you work, start the movie and choose the picture-in-picture option in the iMovie software.
- **Sideline streaming.** There are Picture-in-Picture options for Netflix on Mac and Hulu. While working, you can watch all your favorite programs on Hulu and Netflix, or maybe simply stream several videos at once.
- **Working while in virtual meetings.** Have you ever joined a video conference using a browser and wished you could multitask without closing the browser window? The picture-in-Picture mode might be useful. While everyone else chats, use PiP to hover over your video and keep working.

Picture in Picture in Safari: How to Use

Here are the how-to tips for Picture-in-Picture capabilities in Safari, Chrome, and Firefox if you want to view movies in a browser while using other tabs to carry out your regular tasks.

How to use YouTube's Picture in Picture feature in Safari

The steps:

1. Start your Mac's **Safari** browser.
2. Use **Safari** to visit youtube.com
3. Select the video that you want to see.
4. Do two right-clicks on the video.
5. Choose "**Enter Picture in Picture.**"

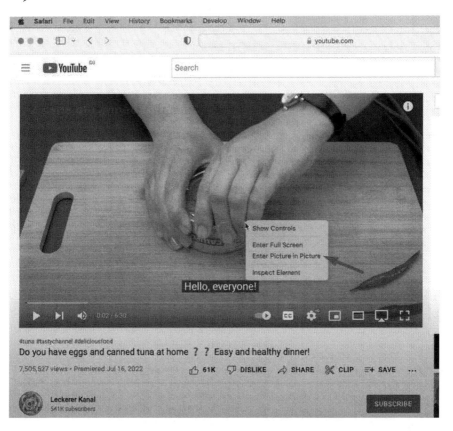

How to access the playback menu's Picture in Picture mode

- Some video players feature their Picture-in-Picture mode, such as YouTube. It is referred to as a "mini player" on YouTube.

- You will enter PiP mode if you click on that icon. Remember that certain options may not be native to PiP and you might not have all the power you want.

Access Picture in Picture from the Address Bar

- A few video hosting services, such as Vimeo, do not allow right-clicking to enter PiP mode and do not provide a native Picture in Picture option.

- Simply right-click the volume symbol in the URL bar of the video you want to watch in PiP. When you do this, a menu will appear with the option "**Enter Picture in Picture**" on it.

Enter Picture in Picture Mode Using a Safari Extension

The steps:

1. Open **Safari on your Mac** and choose it from the menu bar.
2. Select "**Safari Extensions.**"
3. Type "**picture in picture**" into the Mac App Store app that appears.
4. Decide which extension you want to use.

How to use Google Chrome's Picture-in-Picture mode

You can also use Chrome's Picture-in-Picture feature because it's a popular browser.

How to use Chrome's Picture-in-Picture mode to watch YouTube

The PiP settings in Chrome are somewhat similar to those in Safari. In tiny floating windows, it's simple to view YouTube videos:

1. Access YouTube and play the video.
2. Right-click the video twice while holding down the Control key.
3. Click the **Picture in Picture** option.

Use the following technique to watch movies in a mini player while surfing YouTube, which functions much like a video preview:

1. Access YouTube and play the video.
2. Select **Mini player** by clicking the button in the bottom right corner.
3. Keep exploring and browsing on YouTube.

Using Picture in Picture in Firefox

1. Launch **Firefox**.
2. Select the menu option (three horizontal lines on the top right of the Firefox app window)
3. Click on "**Settings.**"

4. Select "**Enable picture-in-picture video controls**" from the "**Browsing**" menu.
5. Open the YouTube video in Picture-in-Picture mode, then click the button in the bottom right corner to activate the feature.

Chapter 17

How to Set up and Use Universal Control in MacBook Air

Use one keyboard, trackpad, or mouse to operate all devices with Universal Control while keeping their operating systems and transferring information across them. **Universal Control** makes a more productive workplace possible.

Device Compatibility

Universal Control can be used with up to two additional devices. That means you can use it with a Mac and two iPads, a Mac and three iPads, or a Mac and three Macs. You should first determine if your devices are compatible with macOS 12 Monterey and iPadOS 15.4 if you haven't upgraded them yet.

macOS 12 Monterey is supported by the following Macs:

- Apple Mini (2018 and later)
- iMac (2017 or later)
- iMac (Retina 5K, 27-inch, Late 2015)

- iMac Pro.
- Mac Pro (2019 and later)
- MacBook (2016 and later)
- MacBook Pro (2016 and later)
- MacBook Air (2018 and later)

These iPads are compatible with iPadOS 15:

- iPad (6th generation and later)
- iPad Air (3rd generation and later)
- iPad Mini (5th generation and later)
- iPad Pro (all models).

Upgrade your iPad and MacBook Air

If your configuration supports Universal Control, ensure all the devices are running the most recent version of their respective operating systems. (i.e. MacOS, iOS and iPadOS). Before updating, don't forget to back up your data.

1. Click the Apple menu, choose **About This Mac**, and you'll see the precise version your Mac is now using displayed under macOS 12 Monterey.
2. You can also go to **System Preferences > Software Update**, which will state that your

Mac is up-to-date if you're already running macOS 12 Monterey or above. If not, a button to **"Update Now"** will appear (or Upgrade Now). When you click on it, the download and installation process will start.

3. Go to **Settings > General > Software Update** on your iPad to see what version it is running. Tap the most recent version, iPadOS 15.4, and choose **Download and Install**.

Installing Universal Control

A couple more conditions need to be met before you can activate **Universal Control**. Make sure **two-factor authentication** is enabled and the **same Apple ID** is used to sign in on all your devices.

In addition, Wi-Fi, Bluetooth, and Handoff must all be switched on, and the devices must be within 30 feet (10 meters) of one another. Finally, your Mac mustn't be sharing its internet connection with other devices (and your iPad isn't using a hotspot to share a cellular connection).

When you're done, follow these instructions to enable Universal Control on your Mac:

1. Go to Settings, then choose **Displays**.
2. Select "**Universal Control.**"

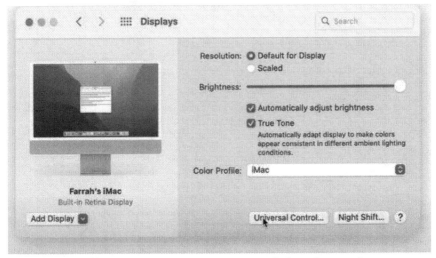

3. Select **Allow your cursor and keyboard to move between any nearby iPad and Mac**.

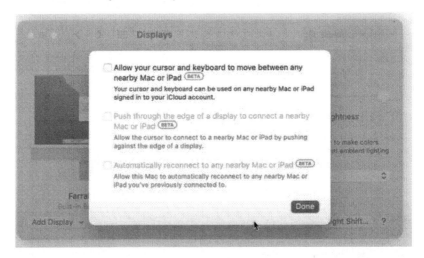

Two other options are available in the same pop-up: "**Automatically reconnect to any nearby Mac or**

iPad" and "Push through the edge of a display to connect to a nearby Mac or iPad."

When you move the pointer over, your Mac will connect to a different device if the first one is switched on. The latter merely causes the devices to reconnect themselves anytime they are close to one another.

Enable Universal Control on the iPad

1. Click **Settings**, then choose **General**.
2. Select **AirPlay and Handoff**.
3. Choose **Keyboard and Cursor**.

Manually activate Universal Control by heading to *Control Center > Display*, selecting your iPad or Mac under the Link Keyboard and Mouse area, and unchecking automatic connectivity.

Using Universal Control

Place the devices side by side after Universal Control is turned on to connect them (they should be unlocked and awake). Next, using your mouse or trackpad, move the Mac's pointer to the left or right edge of the screen in the direction of the linked iPad or Mac. The connection is successful if you can move the pointer back and forth between the displays.

You can place the Mac and iPad exactly to fit your configuration, just as with other external screens. Select **System Preferences > Displays** and manually drag the second Mac or iPad to the left, right, above, or below. This will make using both displays seem much more natural. If you are unable to navigate between a second (or third) display:

1. Launch **System Preferences** on your Mac, then choose **Displays**.
2. Select **Add Display**.
3. Select **Link Keyboard and Mouse** from your iPad's or Mac's menu.

Universal Control is the best method for transferring files and information across two Apple devices while using just one keyboard and mouse. However, it was not designed to replace SideCar because it cannot be used to slide programs or browser windows back and forth between the two devices since it does not enlarge the display of your Mac.

Some features of the Universal Control include:

- Drag images from your Mac to iMessage or the Photos app on your iPad. You can drag files from one Mac to the other if you're using **Universal Control** with a second Mac, and you can also drag files from the Mac to the iPad Files app. Additionally, you can create sketches on your iPad with the Apple Pencil and then drag those sketches into Keynote on a Mac using your mouse.
- You can copy and paste from the Mac to the iPad using keyboard shortcuts or trackpad and mouse motions (**Command-C** to copy on one device and **Command-V** to paste on the other).

How to Disable Universal Control

- There are many methods to disable **Universal Control**. You can choose the linked iPad or Mac by going to **Control Center > Displays** and clicking on it.
- Universal Control will instantly disconnect if you lock your iPad or put your Mac to sleep.

How to Use iPad as a Sidecar

Thanks to Sidecar, you can use your iPad as a second screen for your MacBook Air. With all that additional screen area, you'll work even more effectively, and it's simple to set up. There are ideal scenarios to use Sidecar:

- An appropriate MacBook equipped with macOS 12 Monterey.
- A compatible iPad running iPadOS 15 or later.
- Connect both devices to the same WiFi network and Apple ID.
- Enable Handoff and Bluetooth.
- Ensure that the internet connections of the two devices are not shared.

Setting up Sidecar

Sidecar can be used without an actual cable connection between your iPad and Mac, but both must be logged in with the same Apple ID.

The steps:

1. On your Mac, click **Displays** 🖥 under **Apple menu** 🍎 > **System Preferences**.

2. Select your iPad from the **Add Display pop-up option** if you aren't already connected to it. Additionally, you can connect by using the Display menu in the menu bar or the Display menu in Control Center ⊟ (if the menu is shown).

Change Sidecar Options

Modify the settings under Display Settings after you've configured your iPad to act as a second display for your MacBook Air 2022.

The steps:

1. On your Mac, select **Displays** ▄, **then click Display Settings** under the **Apple menu** > **System Preferences**.
2. After choosing the name of your iPad, choose from the options below:
   - Select **"Use as"** from the pop-up menu, then decide whether you want to expand or mirror your display or use your iPad as the primary display.

- After choosing to display the sidebar on the left or the right using the pop-up menu, choose **Show Sidebar**.
- Choose **Show Touch Bar** from the pop-up menu and decide whether to display the Touch Bar at the top or bottom of the screen.
- Choose "**Enable double tap on Apple Pencil**."

3. Press "**Done**."

Use Sidecar

The steps:

1. To connect to your iPad, select Display in Control Center or the **Display option** 🖥 in the menu bar (if the menu is shown). The menu bar displays the Sidecar menu ▣. From the Sidecar menu, you can quickly alter how you use an iPad at any moment. For instance, you may reveal or conceal the sidebar and Touch Bar on the iPad, or use it as a mirror or independent display.
2. From there, carry out any of the following options:

- Move windows from your Mac to your iPad by dragging them to the edge of the screen until the iPad's cursor appears. Alternatively, choose **Window > Move to iPad** when using an app.
- Drag windows from an iPad to a Mac by dragging them to the edge of the screen until the Mac displays a pointer. Alternatively, choose **Window > Move Window Back to Mac** when using an app.
- To use the Touch Bar on an iPad, touch any button with your finger or an Apple Pencil. Depending on the application or job, several buttons are offered.
- Tap objects like **menu commands**, **checkboxes**, or **files** with your Apple Pencil while using an iPad. Double-tap the bottom portion of your Apple Pencil to change drawing tools in certain applications if your Apple Pencil supports it (and you checked the box in Display options).
- Use iPad motions to input and modify text and basic actions like tapping, swiping, scrolling, and zooming.

- Switch between the iPad and the Mac desktop: Swipe up with one finger from the bottom border to display the Home Screen on your iPad. Swipe up, pause, and the iPad dock will appear. Swipe up and stop in the screen's middle to see the App Switcher. Swipe up, then press the Sidecar symbol ▦ to return to the Mac desktop.

3. On your iPad, hit the **Disconnect symbol** ◻ at the bottom of the sidebar when you're ready to stop using it.

4. On your Mac, you can disconnect by selecting the active iPad from the Sidecar option in the menu bar.

Chapter 18

How to Use the Continuity Camera

If you want to scan papers or snap a photo of anything nearby, you can use your iPhone, iPad, or iPod touch, and the result will display instantaneously on your Mac. Numerous applications, including Finder, Mail, Messages, and others, have compatibility with Apple's Continuity Camera feature.

Check the System Requirements

When your devices are close to one another and configured with the point highlighted below, the **Continuity Camera** will function:

- The Wi-Fi and Bluetooth capabilities of your Mac, iPhone, and/or iPad are all activated.
- Your iPhone or iPad as well as your Mac are both signed in with the same Apple ID using the two-factor authentication feature.
- You are running macOS 12 Monterey or later, and either iOS 12 or a later version is installed on your iPhone(version iOS 15.6.1) or iPad (iPadOS 15.6.1).

On your Mac, you can use the **Continuity Camera** in the following supported applications:

- Finder
- Keynote 8.2 or a later version.
- Mail
- Messages
- Notes
- Page 7.2 version or later
- TextEdit

Take a Photo

The steps:

1. Launch a program that is compatible with your Mac.
2. Carry out one of the following options:
   - While pressing the Control button, click on the program window where you want the picture to appear. Select **Insert** from **iPhone or iPad > Take Photo** from the context-sensitive menu that pops up when you do so. You can perform this action in a **Finder** window or on the desktop instead.

- Select **Insert from iPhone or iPad > Take Photo from the File menu** (or the **Insert** menu, if the **File** option is unavailable).

3. The Camera app launches on your iOS device - an iPhone or an iPad. Hit ⬤ to take a picture, and then tap the *Use Photo button*. Your image will now be shown in the window of your Mac.

Scan documents

The steps:

1. Launch a program that is compatible with your Mac.
2. Carry out one of the following options:
   - While holding the Control button, click on the program window where you want the picture to appear. Select **Insert from iPhone or iPad > Scan Documents** from the context-sensitive menu that pops up when you do so. You can perform this action in a Finder window or on the desktop instead.
   - Select **"Insert from iPhone or iPad" > "Scan Documents" from the "File" menu** (or the **"Insert" menu**, if that menu is present).

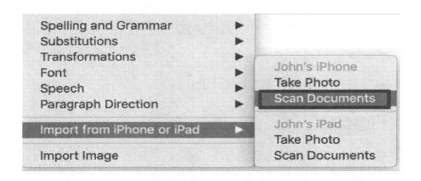

3. The Camera app launches on your iOS device - an iPhone or an iPad. Put the document you want to scan in front of the camera, and then wait for it to complete scanning. If you need to take a scan manually, hit ⬤ or one of the Volume buttons, then drag the corners to modify the scan so that it fits the page, and last, tap the **Keep Scan button**.

4. If you want to add more scans to the document, touch the **Save button** when you are done. The window on your Mac displays the scanned documents as PDF files.

Chapter 19

How to Use Memoji

With the latest macOS 12 Monterey or later, you can make your own Memoji and modify them on your MacBook Air. Memoji enables you to better convey your feelings and moods by using one-of-a-kind stickers tailored to you. Your iMessage exchanges are sure to become more interesting by using this feature.

The Process of Making Memoji Stickers

The steps:

1. Launch the **Messages** application found on the Mac.
2. After that, choose a chat, and then next to the text box, click on the symbol that looks like an app store.

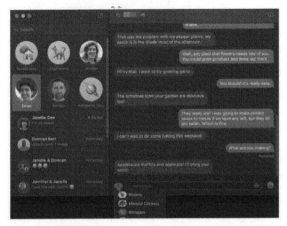

3. Pick out some Memoji Stickers to use.

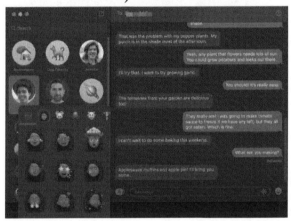

4. In the pop-up window, choose **New Memoji** by clicking on the symbol that looks like three dots.

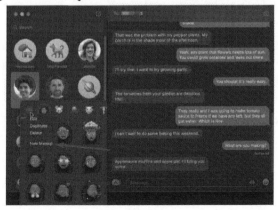

5. You can now have fun creating a Memoji precisely as you want by selecting a unique hairstyle, skin tone, eye color, and several other features.

6. When you are ready, click the **Done button** to create a Memoji that is unique to you. It is now available for usage in conversations and is viewable in the Memojis menu.

How to Change, Replicate, or Delete a Memoji

Once you've created a Memoji, you are free to make changes to it anytime you want. You also have the option of duplicating it or deleting it altogether. The steps:

1. To modify the look of the Memoji, click the icon with three dots and then choose Edit from the drop-down menu.

2. Duplicate the Memoji by selecting the **Duplicate option**.
3. Delete the Memoji by selecting the option from the drop-down menu.

Using Memojis as Your iMessage Group Photo

Choose a Memoji as the profile picture for a group chat, as you would do in Messages on your iPad or iPhone.

The steps:

1. Start by opening the **Messages** app and initiating a group chat. You can alter the name of your group and your profile picture by clicking the "I" **symbol**.
2. Go to the bottom of the page and choose "**Memoji**" **from** the list of available options. You may also choose to see more Memojis by selecting the **See More option**.
3. After that, choose the skin tone you like most for the Memoji, and then click the **Done button**.

How to Change Your iMessage Profile Picture to a Memoji

To send more customized messages using iMessage, you can now use Memojis as your profile picture. In addition, macOS 12 Monterey allows you to choose the individuals who are permitted to see the content that you post. To configure it, follow the procedures that are listed below.

The steps:

1. Open the **Messages app**, then pick **Preferences** from the Messages menu at the top of the screen.
2. Select the option to **Set Up Name and Photo Sharing**.
3. Select the **Continue option**.
4. At this point, choose the **"Customize" option**.
5. Choose a Memoji for yourself. To do so, click the **+** icon.
6. Select the skin tone you like most, and click the **Done button**.
7. After that, you will be prompted to confirm whether you want **your Apple ID and My Card in**

Contacts to be changed with the picture you picked. To verify, click the **Use button**.

8. Next, you will get a prompt if you want your name and picture to be shared with your contacts at all times or to be prompted for permission each time your name and photo are shared. After making your selection, be sure you click the **Done button**.

9. The new one will replace the old image. You can modify it once more at any moment by hovering over it and then selecting **Edit** from the drop-down menu that appears.

Chapter 20

How to use Voice Controls on Mac

This function, which can be accessed easily, serves as your assistant and comes in useful for completing various chores using just your voice. People who have trouble moving around will find it very helpful.

How to activate Voice Control

The steps:

1. Select **Apple menu > System Preferences > Accessibility**
2. Select **Voice Control** from the menu in the sidebar.
3. Select the checkbox next to **Enable Voice Control**. Your Mac may finish a one-time download from Apple when you switch on Voice Control for the first time.
4. When **Voice Control** is turned on, an icon of a microphone appears on the screen. This icon represents the mic that was chosen in the **Voice Control** options.

5. Say "**Go to sleep**" or click the **Sleep** button to put Voice Control to sleep and prevent it from listening further. Say "Wake up" aloud or click the button to bring back Voice Control.

How to Use Voice Control

Familiarize yourself with Voice Control by going through the set of voice commands that are at your disposal. Use the phrase "**Show commands**" or "**Show me what I can say**" to activate this feature. The list is contextually dependent; therefore, you may find versions that are not mentioned. Within the Voice Control choices, you have the option to "**Play sound when the command is detected,**" which will make it simpler for you to determine whether or not Voice Control received your sentence as a command.

Basic Navigation

Voice Control can identify several programs, labels, buttons, and other graphical elements on the screen, allowing you to navigate by combining the names of these elements with specific instructions. Here are several examples:

- **Open Pages:** Create a new document by clicking the button labeled "**New Document.**" After that, choose a format for your letter by clicking the button labeled "Letter." Then save your document: "**Save the document.**"
- To compose a new message in Mail, click the "**New Message" button**.
- Enable the Dark Mode by going to the **System Preferences** menu. Click **General**. Click **Dark**. Then you should close the **System Preferences** window by **selecting "Close window" or "Quit System Preferences."**
- Restart your Mac: Click the Apple menu. You can also use the number overlay and say "**Click 8"** instead of "Click Restart."

Number Overlays

You can easily interact with sections of the screen that Voice Control detects as interactive, such as menus, checkboxes, and buttons, by placing number overlays on top of those elements. Simply uttering the phrase "**Show numbers**" will activate the number overlays. Then you only need to pronounce a number to click it.

Interacting with more complicated interfaces, like web pages, is simplified using number overlays. For example, you might say something like **"Search for Apple shops near me"** in your web browser. The next step is to utilize the number overlay to choose one of the outcomes: "Show numbers." Click 64." (If the name of the link is distinctive, you may also be able to click on it without using overlays by saying "Click" followed by the name of the link.)

Voice Control will display numbers for you automatically in menus and any other place where you need to differentiate between things with the same name.

Grid Overlays

Using grid overlays, you can interact with areas of the screen that do not have control or that Voice Control does not detect as clickable.

- You can also display a numbered grid on your screen by saying **"Show grid,"** or you can restrict the grid to the current window by saying **"Show window grid."** Declare a grid number to subdivide that section of the grid, then repeat as many times as necessary to continue refining your choice.

- Simply saying "**Click**" followed by a grid number will cause the object to be selected from behind that number. Or you can say "**Zoom**" followed by the number to zoom in on a specific part of the grid, at which point the grid will automatically disappear. You may also use the grid numbers to drag an item from one part of the grid to another part of the grid.

- To conceal grid numbers, say "**Hide numbers.**" Saying "**Conceal grid**" will hide the grid as well as the numbers.

Dictation

You can continually dictate while the cursor is in a text field, such as a document, email message, text message, or any text field. Dictation is having one's spoken words converted into written form.

- Simply saying the name of the punctuation mark, symbol, or emoji you want to input, such as "**question mark**" or "**percent sign**" or "**happy emoji,**" will cause it to be entered. These may be different depending on the language or dialect.

- You may use instructions such as "**Navigate up two sentences**" or "**Move forward one paragraph**" or "**Pick the previous word**" or "**Select next paragraph**" to move about in the text and select it.

- When formatting text, you can attempt options such as "**Bold that**" or "**Capitalize that.**" If you want your next statement to be formatted as a number, just say the word "**numeral.**"

- You have a wide variety of options available to you when it comes to deleting text. For instance, if you say "**remove that,**" Voice Control will recognize the command and erase anything you have just written. Or say "**Wipe everything**" to delete everything and start afresh.

- Since Voice Control is aware of contextual signals, you can switch between dictating text and giving instructions without difficulty. For instance, if you wanted to dictate and then send a birthday message using Messages, you might say something like "**Happy Birthday**". **Click Send.**"

Create your Voice Commands

The steps:

1. Open the options for Voice Control by saying something like "**Open the settings for Voice Control.**"
2. Either click the Commands button or pronounce the Commands button aloud. The entire list of all available commands is displayed.
3. To add a new command, click the **add button (+) or say "Click add."** The command can then be defined by configuring these parameters as follows:
   - **When I say:** Enter the phrase or word that you would want to be able to utter to carry out the action.
   - **While using:** Select whether or not your Mac will carry out the action only while using a specific application.
   - **Carry Out:** Pick the Task That You Will Carry Out. You can execute an Automator process by opening a Finder item, opening a URL, pasting text, pasting data from the clipboard, using a keyboard shortcut, selecting an item from a menu, or opening a clipboard.

4. To activate or deactivate a command, use the checkboxes that are provided. You can select a command to determine whether additional phrases are compatible with that command. For instance, "**Undo that**" may be used in conjunction with several other expressions, such as "**Undo this**" and "**Scratch that.**"

5. You can simply add a new command by saying "**Make this speakable,**" which is an option. Voice Control will assist you in configuring the new command according to the circumstances in which it will be used. For instance, if you utter this command when an item on the menu is chosen, Voice Control will assist you in creating a command for picking the item on the menu.

Create your Dictation Vocabulary

The steps:

1. Open the options for Voice Control by saying something like "**Open the settings for Voice Control.**"

2. Either click the Vocabulary button or utter the word "**Vocabulary.**"

3. Either click the **plus sign (+)** on the toolbar or say "Click add."

4. In the Text box, type a new word or phrase exactly as you want it to be said.

How to Use Wake Up/Sleep in Voice Control

You can temporarily turn off Voice Control on your MacBook Air by either using the voice command and saying 'Go to Sleep' or by clicking the **Sleep button** located in the little microphone box on the Home screen. Simply saying "**Wakeup**" or clicking the Wakeup button will reactivate voice commands.

Voice Control on the Mac: How to Use It

Once you have activated Voice Control on your Mac, you can use it to carry out various instructions and procedures.

Add and Change the Voice Control Language

The steps:

1. Select **Motor,** then go to the area labeled **Voice Control**.

2. Navigate to the right side of the page and **choose Language** from the drop-down menu.
3. Select the **Customize option**.
4. Select the language you want to use from the list of possibilities, and then click the **"Ok" button**.
5. Voice Control will be updated to include the selected languages (and will download them if they were not previously present).

Create Custom Commands Using Voice Control

The steps:

1. Navigate to the **Voice Control** menu.
2. Click **Commands**.
3. Navigate to the left sidebar and click the plus sign **+**.
4. In the following step, type the command you want to use next to the **"When I speak" area**. All users will have the option to use the voice command activated by default.
5. To restrict it to specific applications, pick the settings for your use, and then act appropriately.
6. Click **Done**.

Delete Custom Commands in Voice Control

The steps:

1. Navigate to the **Motor section** and look for Voice Control. Once you find it, click the **Commands button** on the right side of the window.
2. Select the custom command you want to remove and click its name.
3. Choose ('-').
4. When asked, choose **Delete** from the menu.
5. Return to the Voice Control menu by selecting the **Done** button. Take note that you are unable to remove the built-in voice commands.

Modify the Microphone Settings for Voice Control

The steps:

1. Navigate to **Voice Control** and choose **Microphone** from the drop-down menu next to it.
2. A list of all the audio devices that are currently connected will show on the screen. Choose the path that appeals to you the most.

Enable and make use of the Overlay feature found in Voice Control

The menu option names for Overlay use numbers since it is a relatively new addition to Voice Control. As a result, you will have an easier time interacting with the various elements of the screen on your Mac. Simply provide the designated number, and you are done. You can use it by turning it on as shown in the following steps:

1. In the right sidebar of **Voice Control**, next to the pull-down menu labeled **Overlay**, click the down arrow.

2. The option will have **none** selected by default. Alter it so that it reads either **Item Numbers** or **Numbered Grid**.

   - **Item Numbers**: When you select this option, a unique number will be assigned to every piece of actionable text or icon that appears on the screen. This includes things like menus and dialog boxes. Simply reciting the number will cause the action to be carried out.

   - **Numbered Grid**: When you choose this option, the screen of your MacBook Air (or the currently active window) will be partitioned into a grid. Simply reciting the corresponding number will allow you to interact with a different portion of your screen.

3. You have several options at your disposal, such as the ability to zoom in or drag a photo.

Note that you can use the voice commands that are listed below:

1. Say "**Show numbers**" to activate the Overlay feature.
2. Use the "**Show grid**" or "**Show window grid**" command to activate the Numbered Grid (for displaying the grid on the active window).
3. Say "**Hide Grid**" to hide not just the grid but also the numbers.
4. Say "**Show numbers**" to activate the Item Numbers feature.
5. To hide numbers, just use the phrase "**Hide numbers.**"

How to disable the Voice Control feature

The steps:

1. Navigate to the **System Preferences menu** under the Apple ⬛ menu.
2. Navigate to the **Accessibility tab**.
3. From the sidebar, choose **Voice Control**, and then clear the checkbox next to **Enable Voice Control**.

Chapter 21

How to Use the Reminder App

When you want to be sure you don't forget anything, reminders are helpful, but far too often, you need a reminder for the same item more than once at various times.

Repeating notifications are incredibly helpful, whether you need one each month to remind you to pay your credit card bill or vehicle payment or one every week to remind you that you're being paid and should stop by the bank before buying supper for the family.

How to Set Up Recurring Reminders

The method of setting repeated reminders on a MacBook Air is straightforward. You just need to set up a repeated reminder on one of your Apple devices. All of your other Apple devices that share the same Apple ID will immediately sync with it.

To set up a recurring reminder on a Mac, follow these steps:

1. Open the **Reminders app** on your Mac, and then click the **+ icon** in the upper right corner to add a new reminder.

2. Click the **info I button** after moving the cursor over the reminder.

3. Select a day and time by checking the **On a day box**.

4. Select the repeat label option from the drop-down menu. Choose the time interval at which the reminder should recur. You can choose from daily, weekdays, weekends, weekly, fortnightly, monthly, every 3 months, every 6 months, or annually. Additionally, a custom interval can be set up.

5. Optionally, you can choose **never or set** "end repeat" to a specific date.

6. Press the return key if you are satisfied with your choice.

How to Set Up Assigning Tasks

The steps

1. In the lower-left corner of Mac's Reminders software, choose **Add List**.
2. Make a new list that you'll use for all the jobs you've been given.
3. Hover over the list and choose the icon of someone.
4. Click **Add People** from the dialog box that displays.
5. Select AirDrop, Mail, Messages, or Copy Link.
6. Click **Share** to share a link to your new list with the recipient.

These methods allow another Apple user to access and use your Reminders list, including the capacity to read from and write to it.

How to Assign a Task to Another Person

The steps:

1. Select the assignment you want to complete.

2. Select the person icon to the left of the **Add Date line**.
3. Select a person from the list of those permitted to see this list.
4. People will be notified after you give a job to them, reminding them that they now have work to accomplish. On your end, the assignment title will include their picture or initials.
5. You can still finish and cross the item off the list even if you delegate it to someone else. Regardless of who marks the reminder as completed, it will vanish from the list.

You cannot delegate work to more than one individual. However, you may reassign it to someone else the same way you did the first time.

Here:

1. Select the assignment you want to share.
2. Select the symbol of a person's head on the **Add Date line**.
3. To delete someone, click the **X** next to their name.
4. You can also click on their name to choose a different person from the list of those who are permitted to access your assignments.

Basically, that is all there is to task delegation and assignment in the Reminders app. Although it's a great tool, you probably won't be able to use it for more difficult collaborative assignments where several individuals must work on a job or if you need to monitor a project's milestones. Despite this, the Reminders app is still a fantastic choice for families, small teams, and couples.

How to Share a Reminder List

You may share reminder lists with other iCloud users who have updated their reminders in your upgraded iCloud reminders account. Anyone with access to the list may add and remove reminders using any iCloud-enabled computer or device. Create a reminder to remind you at a certain time or location, but it won't remind anybody else because notifications are not shared.

You can add or delete recipients from a reminder list after you've begun sharing it, and stop sharing the list with anybody. Reminders may also be sent to those who have access to the list.

Share a List

The steps:

1. Click the **Share option** 👤 after choosing a reminder list in the sidebar of the Reminders. The share button pops up only when the list is being shared or when the cursor is hovered over.

2. If you want to let individuals you add to the list share it with others, select or uncheck the "**Anyone may add additional persons**" item.

3. In the Share List box, choose the invitation-sending method you want to use:
   - To send an invitation using Mail or Messages, choose Mail or Messages, click **Share**, then input the recipients' names before clicking **Send**.
   - To share an invitation through a link or AirDrop, click **Copy Link or AirDrop**, input the recipients' names or phone numbers and then click **Share**.

4. To access and change the shared list, the invitee must consent to the invitation.

Add People to a Shared List

You can add additional individuals to a reminder list once you begin sharing it.

The steps:

1. Click the **Share option** 👤 after choosing a reminder list in the sidebar of the Reminders app on your Mac.
2. If you want to let individuals you add to the list share it with others, select or uncheck the **"Anyone may add additional persons"** item.
3. Click **Add People** in the People window.
4. In the Share List box, choose the invitation-sending method you want to use:
   - To send an invitation using Mail or Messages, choose Mail or Messages, click Share, then input the recipients' names before clicking Send.
   - To send an invitation through a link or AirDrop, click **Copy Link or AirDrop**, input the recipients' names or phone numbers and then click **Share**.

Change who can Share the List with Others

The steps:

1. Click the **Share option** after choosing a reminder list in the sidebar of the Reminders app on your MacBook Air.

2. Choose one of the following actions in the People window.

   - **Permit everyone or no one to add more people:** The "Anyone may add persons" checkbox can be selected or deselected. Except for the list owner, every list member is subject to this setting.

   - **Make it possible for certain people to add other people:** Choose a person from the list, click the **Options button** to the right, and then choose to **Make It Possible for Specific People** to **Add Other People.** This causes a checkbox to show next to the option.

   - **Prevent some persons from adding more people:** To remove the checkmark, choose a person from the list by clicking the **Options button** to the right and then selecting **Allow to Add Other People.**

3. Press "Done."

Remove or Delete People from a Shared List

You can delete someone off the shared list if you no longer want to share a list with them.

The steps:

1. Click the **Share option** 👤 after choosing a reminder list in the sidebar of the Reminders app on your MacBook Air.
2. Choose the person you want to delete in the People window.
3. Choose to **Remove Access** from the Options menu ••• at the right.
4. Press "**Done.**"
5. The shared list is deleted from all of the other person's devices when you remove someone from it.

Stop Sharing a List

You can stop sharing a list with everyone if you decide against it or no longer need to.

The steps:

1. Click the **Share option** 😀 after choosing a reminder list in the sidebar of the Reminders app on your Mac.
2. Click **Stop Sharing**, then click **Continue** in the People box.
3. The list is deleted from all participants' devices when you stop sharing it.

Add or Change Reminders

Add reminders for tasks, projects, shopping, and other things you want to remember. To better organize your lists, use subtasks. For instance, group your shopping list by supermarket aisle. All your Apple devices that you set up with the same accounts now display your new reminders and updates.

Add a Reminder

Fields for the date, location, tags, and flag are accessible for speedy input when adding reminders to a list.

The steps:

1. Choose a reminder list from your Mac's sidebar in the Reminders app.

2. Select "**Add**" ✝ in the top-right corner.
3. Type a reminder title here.
4. Then carry out any of the below options:

- **Add a note:** Below the reminder text, type a note. To add a new line to the message, press **Option-Return**.

- Remind yourself of a day and time by clicking **Add Date**, selecting a recommended date, or clicking **Custom** to choose a date using the calendar. After entering a date, you may click **Add Time** and then choose one of the recommended times. The reminder is an all-day reminder if you don't set a time.

- Keep the following in mind when you enter or exit a location: Select a proposed place by clicking **Add Location**, or enter a location's name to see suggested locations as you type.

- Reminders can be tagged by clicking the **Tag** button, selecting an existing tag, or clicking **New Tag** to create and apply a new tag.

- To mark a reminder, use the **Flag icon**.

- Press **Return** after each reminder you input to add more.

    Siri: Use a phrase like:

- "Don't forget to get light bulbs"
- "Add apples to my shopping list"

Add a Reminder Using Natural Language

Use natural language to speed up the creation of reminders.

The steps:

1. Choose a reminder list from the sidebar in the Reminders app.
2. Select **Add** ┼ from the menu in the top-right position.
3. Add the date or time you want to be reminded when typing the reminder. Take Maris to choir practice on Wednesday at 5 p.m., rent a movie on Friday at 4 p.m., or pay bills on Saturday, may be on the reminder.
4. Select a recommended date.

Change or Add more Reminder Details Using the Inspector

You can edit or add extra information to a reminder after you've created it using the inspector. The inspector offers options you may use to set up repeated reminders, be reminded when messaging a person, and add a URL or picture to a reminder in addition to the date, time, and location information.

The steps:

1. Click the **Info button** ⓘ after hovering the cursor over a reminder in the Reminders app on your Mac.

2. Perform any of the next options:
   - Modify the reminder's heading: Type new text after selecting the existing content.
   - Add a note: Below the text of the reminder, type a note.
   - To tag a reminder, first choose a tag by clicking the **Add Tags box** or create a new tag.
   - To mark a reminder, use the **Flag icon**.
   - To be reminded of a specific day and time, select the **Remind Me on This Checkbox**, click the date, then either choose the date from the calendar or input it into the month, day, and year boxes. Select the **At a Time option** after entering the date, and then enter the time in the hour and minute columns. You can also leave this item unchecked to make the reminder valid all day.

- Place the cursor over the repeat area, click the pop-up menu, then choose an option if you wish to be reminded regularly. Place the cursor over the end repeat field, choose **On Date** from the pop-up menu, select a date from the calendar or input it into the month, day, and year fields to establish an end date for the repeating schedule.
- Keep the following in mind when you enter or exit a location: Choose the **At a Location** checkbox, enter a location in the Enter a Location area, pick a recommended location by typing it, and then choose between **Arriving** or **Leaving**.
- Remember to select the **When Messaging a Person option**, click **Add Contact**, and then choose the recipient.
- To change the priority, hover the cursor over the field and choose an option from the pop-up menu that appears. The reminder list uses exclamation points to denote priority: one for low, two for medium, and three for high.
- Add a URL by selecting the URL column and entering the website address.

- To add pictures, click **Add Image, choose Photos**, pick one or more pictures, and then drag the pictures onto the reminder. You may also opt to snap a picture, scan a document, or add a doodle if an iPhone or iPad is handy.
- Reminders for locations you often visit, such as your home or place of employment, may be quickly created by adding those locations to your Contacts card. The addresses on your card are then included in the proposed list of places when you create a location reminder.

Chapter 22

Set Up and Use Apple Pay on Mac

Add a credit, debit, or prepaid card to the Wallet app on your iPhone, Apple Watch, or any device compatible with Apple Pay. This will allow you to set up Apple Pay.

You will need the following to use Apple Pay:

- A MacBook device compatible with the service and running the most recent version of macOS 12 Monterey or later.
- A supported card.
- An Apple ID that is currently logged in to iCloud.

Setting Up Apple Pay in Safari

Apple's Safari is the application you will need to use on your Mac to complete an online payment. Apple Pay gives you access to various payment choices, and safari is the browser that gives you that access. To complete the transactions, you must first check that the browser you will be using is functional and prepared to start Apple Pay. The following is a list of the steps that should be followed to assist in setting up Apple Pay.

1. On the display of your Mac, begin by opening the Safari web browser.
2. In the menu bar, choose **Preferences** to make any necessary adjustments to Safari.
3. Navigate to the **Privacy option** inside the settings menu.
4. Go to the **Privacy page** and check the box next to **Apple Pay and Cards**. Then, let the website check **Apple Pay and Cards for you**.
5. After completing the setup, you can use Apple Pay to complete transactions whenever it is most convenient for you.

Managing Your Apple Pay Cards on Your Mac

On macOS 12 Monterey, using Touch ID in the system preferences allows you to configure and manage Apple Pay on your personal computer. This will enable you to check on the specifics of the transaction, including your billing address, bank account number, and other contact information. It is essential for you to maintain an accurate record of all of your transactions and to be able to adapt to changing circumstances as they emerge.

The steps:

1. To access the **system preference**, choose it from the menu bar or find it in the programs folder.
2. Select **Wallet and Apple Pay** from the drop-down menus, then open the appropriate window.
3. Open the card in the sidebar to see the specifics of your transactions, including your bank's billing address, account number, and contact information.

If you are using a previous version of Apple Pay on your Mac, and transactions are approved using either your Apple Watch or your iPhone, the only device that will allow you to manage your Apple Pay cards is your iPhone.

Here:

1. On your iPhone, go to the **Settings menu**.
2. To use **Apple Pay**, go to your **wallet** and select it.
3. To see all of your transactions, as well as your billing address and bank account information,

open the appropriate card in the sidebar. This will provide you with access to all of these details.

Setting a Card as Default for Apple Pay

When using several different cards linked to your Apple Pay Card on your Mac, you can choose which card acts as the default at any given moment. This decision could be influenced by the amount of money you have available or by some other aspect of your finances. This is determined based on the user's preferences in the system.

The following information can be useful if you are working with a Mac equipped with a Touch ID.

The steps:

1. To access the system preferences, choose "**System Preferences**" from the **Apple menu** bar or the **Application** folder.
2. Select the **Wallet and Apple Pay option** from the drop-down menu.
3. From the drop-down menu, choose the card that you would want to have set as your default card.

When using an Apple Watch or iPhone on an earlier Mac that does not have Touch ID, it is possible to alter the card set as the default.

1. Navigating to the **Settings app** on your iPhone or Watch.
2. To use Apple Pay, open the **Wallet app**.
3. To choose your default payment method, select the bankcard that you want to use.

Remove a Card from Apple Pay

It is possible to delete a card from **Apple Pay** on your MacBook Air in the same way you add a card to your Apple Pay wallet. This is a possibility while using Touch ID on the Mac, as well as when using an iPhone or an Apple Watch.

The steps:

1. To change the system's settings, open the **preferences** from the menu bar or the program folder.
2. Open the appropriate window by selecting **Wallet and Apple Pay** after clicking on those options.
3. To delete the card, click on it first.

4. To get rid of the sidebar, press the minus sign (-) at the bottom of the page.

5. To verify, choose the **Delete option** from the drop-down menu.

6. Your card has been successfully removed, and you will no longer be able to use it to make online payments using the Apple Pay program that is installed on your Mac.

Chapter 23

How to Use Widgets on Your Mac

You can keep track of your schedule, favorite devices, the weather, top news, and more directly from your desktop by adding and customizing widgets in the Notification Center on your MacBook Air. You can also access the Notification Center by either clicking the date and time, in the menu bar or swiping left with two fingers starting from the right edge of the trackpad. Simply clicking anywhere else on the desktop will close it.

Add Widgets to the Notification Center

The steps:

1. Launch the **Notification Center application** on your Mac.

2. Click the **Edit Widgets button** located at the bottom of the Notification Center.

3. Look for the widget you want to see in the list of widget categories, and then either search for it or click on the category you want, such as "**Clock.**" There are many sizes available for some widgets; selecting one allows you to get a preview of the information it displays.

4. Position the cursor over the widget in the preview, then click the **Add button** ⊕ to add it to the list of active widgets you currently have available.

5. Simply dragging the new widget higher or lower in the list of active widgets will allow you to reorganize its position in the set. Click the **Remove button** ⊖ located on the new widget if you have concluded that you do not want it.

6. When you are through adding widgets, click the **Done** button located at the bottom of the now active widgets.

Customize Widgets in the Notification Center

The steps:

1. Launch the **Notification Center application** on your Mac.
2. Click the **Edit Widgets button** located at the bottom of the Notification Center.
3. In your collection of currently-running widgets, do any one of the following actions:
   - **Modify the information that is shown by a widget:** To choose a widget, move the cursor over it. If the words **Edit Widget** appear underneath the widget's name, it means that you can modify the information. Click the widget to toggle it. Alter the settings by clicking the highlighted information or selecting other alternatives. To choose a different list of reminders, for instance, you can use the List widget for Reminders by clicking the list that is highlighted. When you are done, you may exit the widget by clicking the **Done** button.
   - **To adjust the size of a widget, do the following:** Control-click a widget, and then choose a

different size from the drop-down menu that appears.

4. When you are through making changes to the widgets, click the **Done** button that is located at the bottom of the active widgets.

Remove Widgets from the Notification Center

If you no longer want widgets to appear in the notification center, you can remove them by following the steps below:

1. Launch the **Notification Center app** on your Mac.
2. While holding down the **Option key**, drag the cursor over the widget that you want to delete, and then click the **Delete** button when you are through.

How to Record your Mac's Screen

Recording the display on your Mac can be quite helpful in various situations. You may want to make a screencast with the instructions for others to follow. Possibly, you are putting together a presentation for a company. Alternatively, you may be interested in creating video notes for your use.

Screen Record Using the Screenshot Utility

You may be tempted to download and install third-party screen recorders on your Mac, but the Screenshot Utility is the most straightforward way to capture the display on your Mac. In addition to taking screenshots, this program also enables you to record screen activity.

1. On your keyboard, you'll need to hit **Cmd + Shift + 5** to launch the utility.
2. You will find two recording choices at the bottom of the window. These options are **Record Selected Portion** and **Record Entire Screen**.
3. If you choose **Record Entire Screen**, an image of a camera will pop up on the screen. If you have more than one monitor, this will come in handy. Simply drag the camera to the part of the screen you wish to record, and then click the button to start the video. If you choose **Record Selected Portion**, you may alter the frame size by dragging the edges of the box

that appears on the screen. You can also move the box to a new location on the screen.

4. You can pick several settings for your Mac screen recording after clicking the **Options button**. This includes selecting the microphone you want to use, where you want to store your recording, if you wish to capture mouse clicks and many other options. To begin the recording, when you are ready to do so, press the **Record button** on your device.

How to Stop Recording Your Mac's Screen and Save It

As soon as the recording is over, you won't be able to see the window for the screenshot program, so you may not know how to stop the recording when it's finished. Instead, you should see a little symbol that looks like a stop sign in the menu bar of macOS. Simply clicking on it will put an end to the Mac screen recording.

1. You can also stop the recording by pressing **Cmd + Control + Esc** on your keyboard. Alternatively, press **Command + Shift + 5**, which will bring up

the screenshot bar and give you a choice to stop recording.

2. The recording will be saved to the desktop, and a preview of it will appear in the screen's lower-right corner while it is still being saved (similar to when you take a screenshot). If you click on this preview, you can watch the whole recording and cut it down to the desired length, if necessary.

Advantages of Recording with a Screenshot Utility

The benefits include:

- The screenshot application has been incorporated into macOS 12 Monterey, which means that it is free to use and does not require the installation of an additional screen recorder.
- Additional features include the ability to display mouse clicks for use in lessons, a timer for use in timed recordings, and a built-in microphone for recording audio; the timer is also included.
- You can instantly use AirPlay or the sharing options inside the video you have captured.

Screen Record Using QuickTime Player

Using QuickTime Player is another technique that may be used to capture the display of your Mac. QuickTime Player also uses the Screenshot utility tool; the only difference is that you do it straight from the QuickTime Player program rather than controlling everything via the Screenshot utility tool.

The steps:

1. Launch the **QuickTime Player application**, and from the top menu bar click **"File"** > **"New Screen Recording"** to begin recording using the software.

2. This will open an overlay that provides you with various choices while recording your screen. Like that of the Screenshot function,

you have the option to either **Record the Entire Screen or Record a Selected Portion of it.**

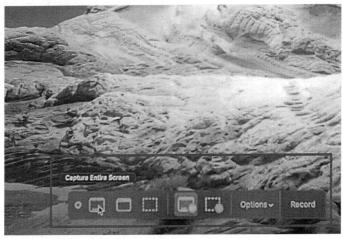

3. After setting up everything, you can begin recording by clicking the **Record button**. You can stop the screen recording by selecting the **Stop icon** from the menu bar.

4. The recorded video will start playing as soon as it's ready. You can change it to meet the requirements (using Trim or Rotate tools). When you are done, go to the **File menu and choose Save** or press the **Cmd key** with the **S key** on your keyboard to save the movie to your desired place.

Advantages of Screen Recording with QuickTime Player

1. QuickTime Player is pre-installed on your Mac, so there is no need to pay for further installation or purchase it separately.
2. Additional functionality, such as simple video editing and audio recording, is available with QuickTime Player.
3. You can instantly use AirPlay or the sharing options inside the video you have captured.
4. QuickTime Player is downloadable for Macs operating earlier versions of the macOS operating system.

Chapter 24

How to Use AirPlay

AirPlay is a feature that enables the streaming, extending, or mirroring of displays, as well as the transfer of material (such as device screens, music, video, photographs, and so on) between devices that are connected to the same local network.

Show the AirPlay Icon on the Menu Bar

To begin the process of streaming via AirPlay, the first thing you will need to do is display the AirPlay symbol on the menu bar of your Mac if it is not already there. You can do this by following the steps outlined below:

1. On your Mac, go to the **System Preferences menu** and choose the **Displays option**.
2. Next, choose the option to **Show Mirroring Options** in the Menu Bar When Available by clicking the checkbox next to it.

How to Use AirPlay on a Mac

There are three different ways to activate AirPlay on a Mac device. You may have to turn on the option to receive AirPlay content on certain of your devices (for example, for an Apple TV, you may have to enable AirPlay in the Settings of the TV and select anyone on the same Network).

Keep in mind that if you want to resize the display of the receiving device, you should use the option "**Match Desktop Size**," regardless of the technique you choose.

Use AirPlay from the Menu Bar

The steps:

1. In the Menu bar, find the symbol that looks like two small toggle switches and click on it to open the **Control Center**. Then, in the menu that appears, choose the **Screen Mirroring option**.
2. After that, in the list of devices, choose the one that will receive the stream by clicking on it (you may have to enter a passcode).

3. You should now see a mirroring symbol in blue on the menu bar. This will remain there until the mirroring session is over. You can enlarge your display size by selecting the option to **Use the Receiving Display as a Separate Display** by clicking on the blue screen-mirroring symbol and then selecting the option from the drop-down menu that appears. You can also move programs to a different display by dragging and dropping them there.

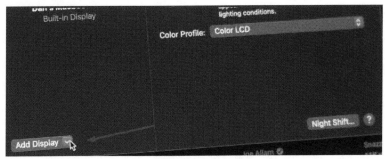

4. When you are done mirroring the screen, click on the blue button that says "**screen mirroring,**" and then pick your device (the device with the blue icon).

AirPlay Audio and Video from Your iPhone or iPad to Your Mac

With the macOS 12 Monterey or later, complete AirPlay capability is now available on Macs. This means that you can now AirPlay content directly from an iPhone or iPad to your Mac, or even from one Mac to another.

After installing the latest macOS, your Mac can serve as an AirPlay 2 speaker source. This will let you stream music or podcasts wirelessly from an Apple device to a Mac, and use the computer as a secondary speaker for multi-room audio.

How to AirPlay Music From an iOS Device to a Mac Computer

The steps:

1. Ensure that your Mac is turned on and that you are logged into macOS with the same Apple account used on your iOS device.
2. Start playing music or podcasts on your iOS devices, such as an iPhone or iPad.
3. In the app's media interface, select the **AirPlay symbol** by tapping it.
4. Select your Mac from the list of devices that are compatible with AirPlay.
5. The audio for your music or podcast should begin playing via the speakers of your Mac or through

any external speakers that are connected to your Mac.

6. You can control playback on your Mac by accessing the Control Center. The symbol for the Control Center can be found in the menu bar at the top right of the screen.

How to AirPlay Videos from an iOS Device to a Mac

The steps:

1. Ensure that your Mac is turned on and that you are logged into macOS with the same Apple account used on your iOS device.
2. Launch a video on your iPhone or iPad and play it.
3. In the app's media interface, select the **AirPlay symbol** and tap it.
4. Select your Mac from the list of devices that are compatible with AirPlay.
5. The movie should begin playing on the display of your Mac, and it should default to full-screen mode. You can exercise direct control over playback on your Mac by clicking on the playback controls that appear on the screen.

Add and Download Music

You can add songs, albums, playlists, and music videos from Apple Music to your music library when you sign up for Apple Music. Your music library will then be available anytime you are logged in to Music on your Mac, iPhone, iPad, or iPod touch.

After you have added songs to your music collection, you can download them to your computer or other devices so that you can play them at any time, even when you are not connected to the internet.

Note: The Apple Songs Voice Plan does not allow for the uploading or downloading of music. Several nations and locations do not have access to Apple Music, Apple Music Voice, lossless, or Dolby Atmos.

Add Music to your Library

The steps:

1. To locate music that you wish to add to your library, open the **Music app** 🎵 on your Mac and perform one of the following:
   - **See specific suggestions that have been made for you:** When you click **Listen Now** in the

sidebar on the left, you will be able to access music that you have recently listened to, customized playlists that have been produced for you, genres that you may like, and other options.

- **Check out the latest additions to Apple Music:** You can search for music based on your mood, recent releases, charts, and more by clicking the **Browse button** in the sidebar on the left.
- Search the Apple Music library.

2. You can add to the songs in your collection by doing one of the following:
    - To add anything, move the cursor over the item you want, then click the **Add button** +
    - To add an item to your library, move the pointer over the item you want to add (for example, a song or album), click the **More button** ⋯, and then select **Add to Library**.
    - To add the item to the sidebar, drag it there. When you drag a song, for instance, you can add it to the library or a particular playlist instead.

Note: If you add an Apple Music playlist to your library, the songs in the playlist are updated whenever the playlist owner changes them. However, the individual songs do not display in your list of songs. This happens when you add a playlist to your library.

3. If you do not see these options, you are either not logged in to Apple Music using your Apple ID, you have not joined Apple Music, or the Sync Library option in Music preferences is not chosen. To check: Select **Music > Preferences**, then click **General**. Ensure the checkbox next to Sync Library is checked, and click **OK**.

Say something like, "**Add this music to my library**," and then wait for Siri's response.

Download Music to your MacBook Air

The steps:

1. Launch the Music app 🎵 on your Mac, and in the sidebar, choose an option that is located underneath the Library heading. For instance, you can see all of the songs in your collection by clicking the **Songs tab**.

2. Move the cursor over an item, then choose one of the following options to begin downloading

music to your computer that you have added to your music library:

- To download, click the icon labeled "**Download ↓**."

- To download, choose **More** ••• from the menu, and click the **Download option**.

If the song you're downloading is available in Dolby Atmos, the Dolby button ◗◖ will display next to it. Depending on your preference, you'll have the option to download the song in either stereo or Dolby Atmos format. Choose **Songs > Preferences**, click **General**, and then choose the **Download Dolby Atmos tickbox**. This will allow you to download music in Dolby Atmos whenever it is made available.

Chapter 25

How to Create and Customize Voice Recordings

Do you want to hear how amazing you sound when you record your voice? Or do you want to capture another person's voice? With the help of Voice Memos software, recording is quite simple, even on a MacBook Air 2022. This function makes it incredibly easy to capture voice recordings and modify them afterward.

Creating Voice Recordings on Voice Memos

The steps:

1. On your Mac, launch the **"Voice Memos"** app.
2. In the lower-left corner of the screen, choose the **red "record" button.**
3. If you want to pause to take a break from the recording, start the recording and click the **"Pause"** button in the bottom left corner.
4. The **"Resume"** button replaces the **"Pause"** button if you want to keep recording. When you are

done recording, choose the "**Done**" **button** in the recording window's lower right corner.

5. Your recording will be stored after you've clicked "**Done**," at which point it will show up in the "**All Recordings**" **section** on the left. Your recordings can also be renamed here.

Editing Voice Recordings on Voice Memos

Tap any recording on your Mac with two fingers and choose "**Edit Recording**" from the pop-out menu to edit it.

Replacing a Section of the Recording

- On the editing screen for recordings, you may make a few modifications. The first and most obvious choice is "**Replace**." With this option, any bit in your recording is essentially replaced with a newly recorded bit.
- This implies that you can change the problematic portion of the recording and avoid having to start over from scratch. Click "**Change**" after dragging the blue line on the recording preview to the beginning of the portion you wish to replace.

- The recorder will start recording again as soon as you **click "Replace."** Before pressing the replace button, ensure you have the ideal component available.
- Click the **"Resume"** button to pick up where you left off with the replacement recording. If not, choose **"Done."**

Trimming a Section of the Recording

- Using the **'Trim' option**, you can also shorten the recording and just save the best parts. On the recording edit screen, click the **"Trim" icon** in the top-right corner to get to this.
- Drag the side handlebars to the portion you want to save. Then choose **"Trim"** to cut off the unwanted part of the recording and just keep what you want.
- If you have cut the proper piece, click **"Save."** If not, choose **"Cancel,"** then repeat the trimming.
- Additionally, you may immediately access the **"Trim Recording" option** from the **"All Recordings" tab**. Tap any recording you want to trim with two fingers, then click the dropdown menu and choose **"Trim Recording."**

Remove a Section of the Recording

- To completely remove a part from the recording, drag the sidebars in that direction and choose the "**Delete**" option.
- The undesirable portion would no longer be present in the recording. If you did a good job, click "**Save**"; if not, click "**Cancel**" and start again.

Creating a Copy of the Same Recording

- This option is referred to as "**Duplicate.**" Create a copy of the same recording if you love it and want to keep a backup of it or a copy where you can experiment with adjustments.
- With two fingers, tap the recording you want to duplicate, and then choose the "**Duplicate**" option from the dropdown menu.

Remove/Delete Background Noise from your Recording

One of the most recent updates to the Mac's "**Voice Memos**" **program** is one that came with the macOS 12 Monterey. You can improve your recording, eliminate background noise, and even smooth the voice memo.

To do so:

1. Click on the "wand" symbol in the upper right corner of the "Edit" page itself, near the "trim" icon.
2. The wand symbol should become blue after you click it. In the bottom right corner of the screen, press the "Done" button.

Chapter 26

How to use Tab Groups in Safari

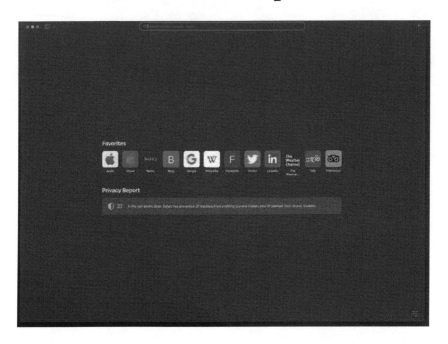

Although Apple may have revised its intentions for Safari tabs in macOS 12 Monterey, Tab Groups are a separate concept and will continue to exist. When you launch your device, you will see that Safari has changed, which could be the most obvious change.

Using the Tab Group Controls

- You will quickly become used to using Tab Groups and detest going back to the ancient era before they existed. However, due to how Safari changes its look, it is challenging to detail the stages. .

- The location of Tab Groups in Safari's Bookmarks sidebar is accessible by clicking on the **Bookmarks icon** next to the traffic lights in the upper left corner. A little arrow to the right of that symbol also indicates the presence of a dropdown menu.

- Any groups are shown when you click on the symbol to enter the Bookmarks sidebar. Additionally, a new button for establishing new groups is included.

- You then get one more tool after creating any Tab Groups and closing this bookmarks sidebar. Click on the name of the current Tab Group next to the Bookmarks symbol to swiftly navigate between various groups.

- The little downward-pointing arrow that was previously placed next to the Bookmarks symbol is now placed next to the name of the current Tab Group.

How to create a Tab Group from scratch in Safari

The steps:

1. In Safari, choose the **Bookmarks icon** by clicking the little dropdown arrow.
2. Select **New Empty Tab Group**.

3. Fill in the name of your new group.

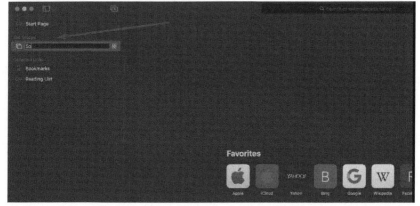

4. Then access any website.

5. You can click on a name in the list or the drop-down menu next to the group name and the bookmarks sidebar icon to switch between various Tab Groups.

Adding a single website to a Tab Group in Safari

The steps:

1. Select a **Tab Group** from the dropdown menu or list.
2. Launch a new tab.

3. Then access the desired website.

How to transfer/move a website in Safari to another Tab Group

The steps:

1. Open the tab you want in a different group if you made a mistake.
2. Next, control-click or right-click on its name.
3. Select **Move to Tab Group**.
4. Choose the group name you want to move it to.
5. That tab is currently in the desired group. There are other options available here. You may right-click a tab, choose **Move to Tab Group**, and then select **New Tab Group** as an alternative. Now, irrespective of whether a tab is already a part of a group, the same option is accessible in every tab.

How to see each tab in a group simultaneously

The Tabs button has been updated with a square icon that has four boxes. There is just one new thing that happens when you click it compared to the previous **Tabs button**.

- Now, Tab Groups also have access to the same Tabs button. To open the sidebar, click the **Bookmarks icon**. Next, click any **Tab Group** to select it.
- When you do so, the new Tabs symbol will appear next to the group's name. When you click it, Safari displays a sizable thumbnail of every tab in that Tab Group.

Following that, you can:

- Use the mouse to choose a tab.
- Press the plus symbol + to add a new tab.
- Look for a tab.

- Click the magnifying glass icon in the upper right corner of any tab thumbnail to search. As you input a search term, Safari will only display the tabs that match what you are searching for.

Close tabs in Safari

You can prevent your window from cluttering several tabs when surfing the web or doing research.

Perform any of the following actions on your Mac's Safari app:

- To close a tab, hover the cursor over it in the tab bar and click the **Close button** ☒ on its left side.
- **Close all open windows**: Select **Close Other Tabs** by selecting Control-clicking the tab you want to remain open.
- **Close all right-hand tabs**: Close Tabs to the Right by selecting a tab with the control key.
- The Back button ⟨ can be used to shut a tab that is opened when you click a link.

Chapter 27

Turn On Mail Privacy Protection

When enabled, Mail Privacy Protection hides your IP address to protect you from malware that may be sent alongside emails. These steps aid in hiding your identity and your online conduct. Without these protections, government agencies, data scrapers or spies might learn crucial details about your whereabouts and online activities. They may include specialized remote material in an email, enabling them to compile specific information. The specifics they may gather are your IP address, the dates and times you see messages, and other information you presumably want to keep secret. Even while some of the information acquired may appear harmless, it is still not ideal to provide your IP address to a possibly hostile operator.

How to Turn on Mail Privacy Protection

When you start the Mail app for the first time after updating to macOS 12 Monterey or a later version, you will be prompted to activate Mail Privacy Protection. However, you can always modify the option in your Mail settings. To activate Mail Privacy Protection, follow these steps in the macOS Mail Settings:

1. Select **Mail > Preferences > Privacy** from the menu.

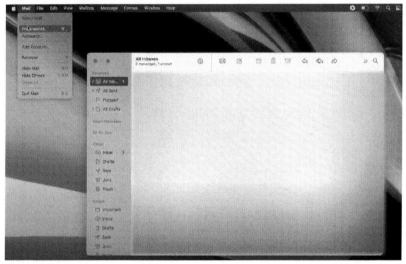

2. Check the box next to **Protect Mail Activity**.

3. Make sure there is a blue check mark next to the "**Protect Mail Activity**" label to deactivate Mail Privacy Protection.

4. Additionally, you can turn on the feature's of various components separately. Uncheck Protect My Mail and choose the relevant settings if you simply want to use **Hide IP Address** or **Block All Remote Content**.

Install and Run Microsoft Windows 11 on a 2022 MacBook Air

The macOS 12 Monterey allows for the installation of Microsoft Windows 11. Some factors can influence your decision to use Windows on a semi-regular basis. Users can install Windows 11 on MacBook Air as an alternative to going out and purchasing a new Windows PC.

How Do Parallels Work?

Without a doubt, using Parallels to install Windows 11 on a 2022 MacBook Air is the best and simplest option. A virtual machine will be set up on your Mac and used to run Windows 11 on your MacBook Air. This allows you to transfer data across the various operating systems without having to physically switch between separate machines, giving you the freedom to use all of the Windows software that you need.

Parallels have been the standard option for anyone wishing to run Windows on a virtual machine for years. So long as you can obtain the ARM version of Windows 11, you should have no trouble installing and using it on a MacBook Air using Parallels.

How To Set Up

The installation procedure is, for the most part, rather simple. There are several Parallels versions available, and each one provides a little something different:

- ($79.99) Parallels Desktop: Standard Edition
  - 8 GB vRAM
  - 4 vCPUs
  - Email and phone assistance for 30 days
- Parallels Desktop: Professional Edition ($99.99 annually)
  - 128 GB vRAM
  - 32 vCPUs
  - Unlimited email and phone support

- Parallels Desktop: Business Edition, which costs $99.99 annually
  - 128 GB vRAM
  - 32 vCPUs
  - Unlimited email and phone support
  - Centralized management and administration

The quantity of vRAM and vCPUs available between the Standard and Pro Editions makes up the difference between them, excluding the Business Edition. Additionally, since you must pay on an annual basis, the Pro Edition is only accessible through subscription. The Standard Edition, which is intended for use at home and by students, is a one-time fee.

The ability to sign up for a free trial is Parallels' finest feature. This enables you to experiment before determining which version is best for you and your requirements.

Follow these instructions to install Windows 11 on a 2022 MacBook Air:

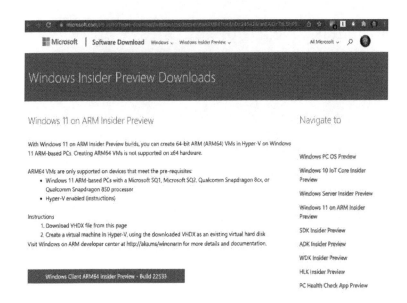

The steps:

1. Download **Parallels'** most recent version on your 2022 MacBook Air.

2. Install it on your Mac after downloading it, then follow the instructions to provide access.

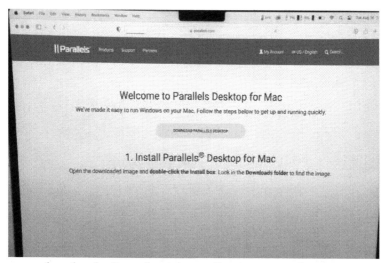

3. Visit the link for the **Windows Insider Preview**.

4. Register for a Microsoft account.

5. Select the button for Windows 11 on **ARM Insider Preview** (Build 22533).

6. Watch for the download of Windows 11 on ARM Insider Preview to be completed.

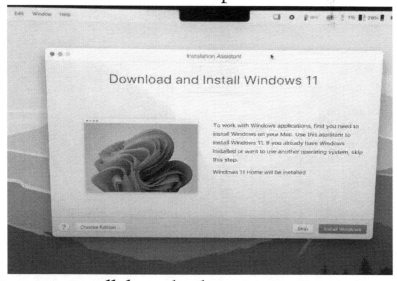

7. Reopen **Parallels** and select **Create New**.

8. To add the Windows ARM file to the Parallels page, drag it there.

9. Press the **Next key**.

10. Select whether you want to use this just for games or productivity and click the **Continue option**.

11. Type a name and the location where you want the virtual machine to be installed, then click **Continue**.

12. Provide access to your Bluetooth devices, microphone, and camera (if appropriate) when requested.

13. Create a **Parallels account** or log in after the installation is complete.

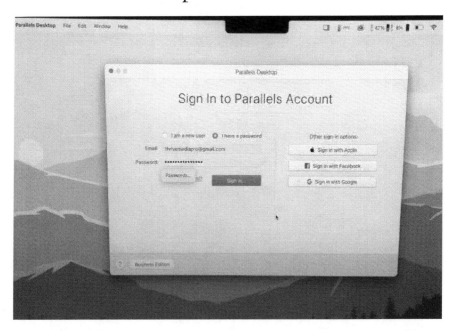

Parallels use your 2022 MacBook Air's resources, so you can decide to make some adjustments. You can choose how many cores are used and how much RAM the virtual machine can use.

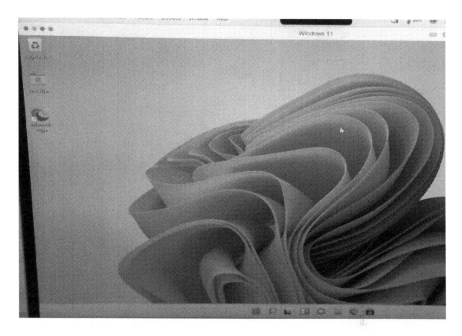

However, it merely depends on how you want to use the virtual machine. If it's for some casual gaming, the suggested settings should work just well. But if you're going to play something more intense, you'll probably want to turn the difficulty up a notch or two.

About the Author

Stanley Lindberg is a Product tester and a tech reviewer. He has reviewed several Apple products. His technological knowledge has seen him earn a job at Apple's headquarters while contributing to the development and advancement of Apple upcoming products.

Made in the USA
Columbia, SC
11 October 2023

24233901R00170